Ben Elton has proved himself the most popular and the most controversial comedian to emerge in recent years. As well as his own stand-up routines, Ben's numerous writing credits include *Blackadder II, Blackadder the Third, Blackadder goes Forth, The Man From Auntie, The Young Ones* and the international bestselling novel *Stark*. *Gasping* is his first play.

Also by Ben Elton in Sphere Books:

STARK (a novel)

GASPING

the play
by
Ben Elton

SPHERE BOOKS LIMITED

A Sphere Book

First published in Great Britain by Sphere Books Ltd 1990

Copyright © Ben Elton 1990.

The right of Ben Elton to be identified as author of this work
has been asserted by him in accordance with the Copyright,
Designs and Patents Act 1988.

Enquiries regarding performance rights to GASPING
should be addressed to McIntyre Management Ltd
15 Riversway, Navigation Way, Preston PR2 2YP

Printed and bound in Great Britain by
BPCC Hazell Books
Aylesbury, Bucks, England
Member of BPCC Ltd.

ISBN 0 7474 0889 0

Sphere Books Ltd
A Division of
Macdonald & Co (Publishers) Ltd
Orbit House
1 New Fetter Lane
London EC4A 1AR
A member of Maxwell Macmillan Pergamon Publishing Corporation

4N 797
7192
LIT

GASPING

Gasping was first performed at the Theatre Royal Haymarket, London, on 1st June 1990. The cast, in order of appearance, was as follows:

PHILIP	Hugh Laurie
SIR CHIFFLEY LOCKHEART (CHIEF)	Bernard Hill
SANDY	Simon Mattacks
MISS HODGES	Catherine McQueen
KIRSTEN	Jaye Griffiths
WEATHER FORECASTER/MINISTER/ REPORTER	Catherine McQueen

With the voice of Stephen Fry

Directed by Bob Spiers. Designed by Terry Parsons. Produced by Philip McIntyre.

ACT ONE

SCENE ONE

The Executive Boardroom of Lockheart Holdings. A power office with large panoramic windows. A strategy meeting is in progress, graphs and charts.
PHILIP *and* SANDY, *two top young exec's, are pitching to* SIR CHIFFLEY LOCKHEART, *the Chief.*

PHILIP: And so Chief, as you can see, all divisions are way way ahead of seasonal predictions. Look (*he takes a graph*) this is my biggest graph and Peter Profit is way way off the right hand corner . . . I've had to glue two together (*he proudly folds it out*) . . . Well obviously *I* didn't do it. I had some of my people do it. Anyway, whoever did it, the results, as I think you'll agree, are impressive. Our corporate hem-line is showing off plenty of stunning thigh. If this keeps up much longer we're going to have to move into a very much bigger pair of corporate trousers. Possibly Switzerland.

CHIEF (*slightly confused by* PHILIP's *language*): Hmm, yes, can I just get this clear Philip. We're making money? Is that what you're trying to say?

PHILIP: Senior money, Chief. If *God* wanted to buy into Lockheart stock, he'd have to think twice *and* talk to his people.

CHIEF: Good. Good, at least I think good. So taking a broad view Philip, charts and presentation rubbish aside, what's your personal gut reaction?

PHILIP (*thoughtfully pacing*): Well Chief, I would have to say, that I am very excited. In fact I have said it, I said it to my people only this morning, 'People,' I said, 'I am very excited,' and they know I don't mince about the bush. But it isn't just me Chief, the sales task force is very excited. The boys in corporate raiding are very excited. The market strike unit damage control spin doctors are very excited. Above all Chief *you* should be excited . . . Sir Chiffley Lockheart should feel like a twelve-year-old who's just discovered it's not only for pissing.

(*A phone rings.* PHILIP *and* SANDY *instantly produce portable phones.*)

PHILIP, SANDY: Not now goddammit.

(*The phone rings again.* CHIEF *calmly picks up one of the phones on his desk.*)

CHIEF: Thank you Miss Hodges, could you possibly hold all calls? Thank you . . . (*crossing to champagne trolley, fingering bottles.*) And you Sandy, how do you feel about our corporate erection? Are you as excited as Philip?

SANDY: Well Chief, I wouldn't want to commit myself fully until I'd talked to my people, but off the cuff, as a non-binding, ball park reaction, I'd say that if anything I was slightly more excited than Philip.

CHIEF: *More* excited?

SANDY: Slightly Sir.

CHIEF: I see. (*pause*) Unfortunately, I'm not.

SANDY: Slightly more excited than Philip in one way
Sir . . . but in twelve other ways, rather less so
(*stifles yawn*) . . .

PHILIP (*surprised pause*): Chief, I'm just not in
following mode here. I mean, look at the graph!
We couldn't be making any more money if we
were a Lesbian couple with six test-tube kids
living off the social security in a Labour
controlled borough while the Home Office tried
to send us back to Sri Lanka.

CHIEF: Please don't misunderstand me Philip. I'm
pleased, good lord yes, oh no question there. It's
just that I'm not excited.

PHILIP: You're not?

CHIEF: I couldn't be less excited if you were both
Swedish.

PHILIP (*pulling himself together*): Chief, you're
absolutely right. OK, so Peter Profit has opened
up his dirty mac and said, 'What about that for a
whopper.' But hell, there are bigger girls in the
cat-house down the street and they can squat
down and pick up ping-pong balls! and, what's
more, without using their hands. We have to
meet Terry Triumph and Derek Disaster and
treat those two impostors just the same.

SANDY: The Chief's right Phil. Champagne? Forget
it, mine's a cup of coffee, very black and I'm onto

my next video ledger heading for the right hand
column with my decimal point in my hand.

PHILIP (*packing up his visual aids*): Sorry to have
wasted your time Chief. We'll be back when this
red line (*the graph*) is wound round the room so
often you'd think it was a Blue Peter Christmas
appeal . . .

(*They are about to go.*)

CHIEF (*stopping them*): Don't be absurd, our profits
are quite magnificent. I'm delighted with them.
But you have to face facts. There is nothing
remotely *exciting* about our present success. We
make our huge piles of money by *having* huge
piles of money. We buy land, take over factories,
invest in other people's labour and creative zeal.

(PHILIP *and* SANDY *are rather crushed.*)

CHIEF (*reflecting for a moment; he has something
significant to tell them*): Gentlemen, I'm no longer a
young man but my life so far has been a full one.
I've seen a great deal and I've bought almost all
of it. I've hobbed with the rich and I've nobbed
with the beautiful. Do you want to know what is
exciting? (*pause*) The Pot Noodle. That's what's
exciting. Find me a Pot Noodle, *then* you shall see
your old Chief excited.

(*There is a brief pause for surprise.*)

PHILIP (*pacing across the room, hits the intercom*): Daphne
get your sweet little ass in here pronto dammit, with
some Norris Noodles, instant variety, assorted
flavours and why the *hell* wasn't this anticipated.
You're paid to *think* goddammit . . .

(*intercom off*) All sorted Chief, I can't imagine how it got overlooked.

CHIEF (*at intercom*): Cancel the last request Miss Hodges. I should explain Philip that I am employing a metaphor . . .

PHILIP: You won't find I have a problem with that Chief, if a guy's good, I don't care where his parents were born.

CHIEF: (*arm round* PHILIP): Philip, come over here, let me show you something.

PHILIP: With you Chief.

CHIEF: It's a painting by Rembrandt, who as you may be aware, was a painter. It is a torso.

(*They cross to wall where a picture hangs.*)

PHILIP (*wishing to convey awe-struck delight*): Oh . . . . . .
Oh Sir, oh oh oh *Chief* . . . . . . it's exquisite Sir, quite exquisite . . . . . . the uhm colour . . . . . . and the . . . . light, yes, that's it, the light. Am I right Sandy? back me up.

SANDY: No question Philip, the guy had senior talent. The sort of rough-hewn, fierce-eyed, canvas-covering cowboy who'd get up in the morning and say to his shaving mirror, 'I *can* paint. I *will* paint.' By mid-afternoon he's holding a major retrospective and he's *bored*.

PHILIP: Exactly! Chief, let me tell you a little about the way I see this guy. Come 5.30 on the West bank of the Seine, when all the other smock-wearers are packing up their brushes ready for another evening of booze, whores, and trying to come to terms with being only three feet tall, friend Rembrandt power-packs another paletteful, phones the Louvre, tells them to clear a wall and before you know it, the *Mona Lisa*'s winking that inscrutable wink at him while her ears dry.

CHIEF: You're an admirer then?

PHILIP: Be a fool not to be Chief. The fact that Rembrandt had access to real business-class ability is *not* negotiable. Christ, you only have to look at the guy's product (*indicating canvas*).

CHIEF: Well you may be right, I'm sure you are, but as it happens, this isn't the picture. This is the picture of the bright purple Spanish girl in the nude that some clever so-and-so sells millions of every year. The Rembrandt's behind it. (*pushes button, picture rises up, to reveal second picture set in wall*) What do you think?

PHILIP: . . . And this one's the Rembrandt is it?

CHIEF: It is.

PHILIP: Oh, oh Chief, oh oh oh *Chief* . . . . . . it's exquisite Sir, quite exquisite . . .

CHIEF: The light and the colour good?

PHILIP: Terrific.

CHIEF: Good, because this pretty little Dutch girl cost me seventy-two million pounds. (*general gasp*) I think they saw me coming, what do you think?

PHILIP: We-ell, I suppose it is a substantial *wad* to lay out for a piccy, but you're a 'can do, must have' kind of guy Sir. Sandy?

SANDY: When Sir Chiffley Lockheart says 'I want', the price tag does *not* have a seat at the negotiating table.

CHIEF: The point I am trying to make gentlemen, is that this (*the painting*) is a Pot Noodle. And this . . . (*takes Spanish picture*) by a matter of coincidence is also a Pot Noodle. Do you want to know what a Pot Noodle is?

PHILIP: Uhm . . . . . . it's a painting?

CHIEF: A Pot Noodle is the most beautiful thing on Earth. It is a new way of making money. A way of making money . . . *where no money existed before*: the very definition of excitement.

PHILIP: Look, I'm probably being thicker than a middle manager's filofax here Chief, but I'm just not in an 'understanding you' mode at all. Uhm . . . . . . what *is* a Pot Noodle?

CHIEF: It's a large plastic cup containing chemically-saturated dried spaghetti and peas to which the consumer is instructed to add boiling water.

PHILIP: Ye-e-s . . . and perhaps you could talk me through the significance factor on this one . . .

CHIEF: The most unlikely food stuff in history. When they launched it nobody gave it a chance . . . Nonetheless, against all expectations the market not only absorbed it, but embraced it. There was no drop in sales of any other form of food. Money had been generated where *no money existed before*.

PHILIP (*very impressed*): And all because of one bonkers, iron-willed troubleshooter who put his balls into a cup of spaghetti.

CHIEF: Only the British could market Pot Noodle, because only the British would eat them. That unknown marketing hero had faith in the concrete, rat-like digestive system of the British consumer and he's been in profit since day one.

PHILIP: My God Chief, that's probably the most inspirational anecdote I've come across since I first leafed through my Gideon in a Holiday Inn.

CHIEF: Pot Noodles come in all shapes and sizes. This picture is worth seventy-two million because that's what I paid for it, nothing to do with its intrinsic value. There's probably more light and colour in a packet of fruit-flavoured Polos. What makes the thing so special is that when I sell it the bidding will *start* at seventy-two million. This (*the Spanish painting*) is a Pot Noodle . . . Who could possibly have predicted that anyone would want anything so ugly, and yet some brilliant fellow thought of printing them onto hardboard and getting Woolworth's to stock them next to the Pick'n'Mix. Anyone worth their company BMW can carve a bigger share of an existing market, but show me the person who can make a pound where there was *no pound to be made*. That's the fellow who's going to be sitting alongside me and the board in the executive Jacuzzi whirlpool bath.

PHILIP: The executive Jason Chief, that's a mightily big carrot!

CHIEF: Find me a Pot Noodle and you're in it Philip, what's more you can sit on one of the jets. Find me a Pot Noodle!! Bring the excitement back! Make me some money where no money existed. Make an old man happy!!

SCENE TWO

Cut to darkness.
The sounds of a squash court, the huge grunting of the
players, the banging of the ball, followed by anguished
shouts of self-loathing.
(*HUR!-BONK HUR!-BONK HUR!-BONK . . .*) Hell
   bugger-it!!
(*HUR!-BONK HUR!-BONK HUR!-BONK . . .*) Oh
   for *Christ's* sake what the *hell* am I *doing!*
(*HUR!-BONK HUR!-BONK HUR!-BONK . . .*) Come
   on, God I'm playing like a *total prat.*
(*HUR!-BONK HUR!-BONK HUR!-BONK . . .*)
   Bollocks!

(SANDY *and* PHILIP *front of stage in squash gear, they*
put their phones down. They have rackets but they mime
the ball. They face outwards towards the audience who
are the back wall.)

PHILIP: Well I must say I'm looking forward to a
   couple of punishing points of 'wallop the bollock'
   eh Sandy?

SANDY: In likewise mode Philip!

(*They warm up etc.*)

PHILIP: Feeling pretty trim actually – by bugger I've
   pumped so much iron lately you could melt me

down and beat me into a canteen of cutlery.

SANDY: I'll lob one up shall I?

PHILIP: Give it your best shot young Sandy.

SANDY (*mimes a hard serve with a grunting*): Huuurrrr!!

PHILIP (*mimes a return with an even bigger*):
Huuurrrrrrrr!!!

(PHILIP *bobs about as if ready to return again, but*
SANDY *has relaxed and is looking behind him at the
ground. It is clear that despite* PHILIP's *huge lunge and
grunt, he missed his shot completely.*)

SANDY: Out.

PHILIP (*realizing*): Hmmm, yes, I suppose *technically* it
is, yes, not bad Sandy, not bad at all, but you're
putting far too much curve on it. Try to imagine
that there's an invisible string attaching your right
wrist to your left ear. Here, look, I'll show you.
(*he picks up the imaginary ball and plays shot with
huge grunt,* SANDY *returns,* PHILIP *lunges, grunts and
misses again*) You forgot the string Sandy, you're
not concentrating are you? You'd better serve,
give you the edge.

SANDY: Right you are, love all then.

PHILIP: Love all it is. (SANDY *is about to serve,* PHILIP
stops him) Of course I can't blame you for being
off your stroke after the session we had with the
Chief this morning. He certainly is an inspiration.

SANDY: Mmm. So it's love-all.

PHILIP: And not likely to change until you serve, old
scout.

SANDY (*gives him a look and then serves*): Hurrr
(*BONK*).

PHILIP: I mean, working the . . . (*ball hits wall BONK*)
kind of hours I do . . .

(PHILIP *returns BONK . . .*)

PHILIP: . . . a fellow needs a passion . . . (*ball hits wall
BONK*) for some people there's always birds I
suppose . . .

(SANDY *returns BONK.*)

PHILIP: . . . but not me I've no time for totty (*ball hits
wall BONK*) . . . Ha!!!

(PHILIP *makes huge lunge and swipe, and misses. The
ball goes Dibbly Dibbly.*)

SANDY: One-love.

PHILIP: Mmmm, did you see what I was trying to
show you there? Cross-court wrong foot, well
worth picking up.

SANDY (*picking up ball and preparing serve*): One-love.

PHILIP: Technically yes.

SANDY(*serves*): Hurrrr (*BONK*).

PHILIP: Quite frankly . . . (*ball hits wall BONK*) . . . if
I do make totty time . . .

(PHILIP *hits ball BONK.*)

PHILIP: . . . the ruddy girl's . . . (*ball hits wall BONK*)
always busy. Amazing . . .

(*It was a lob*, SANDY *watches it land, turns round and
plays it off back wall BONK . . .*)

PHILIP (*turning round as well*): Ah, now your problem is . . . (*Ball hits wall BONK. They both turn out again . . . ball goes Dibble Dibble.*)

SANDY: My point.

PHILIP: Ye-es, but it could so easily not have been . . . I played my drop plonker shot into your gutter.

SANDY: Two-love (*walking forward to pick up ball*).

PHILIP: So there you were with my plonker in your gutter and you go to pieces, start looking the wrong way and God knows what. Can't blame you really, it is pretty disconcerting when one considers just how ruddy busy girls are these days. Sometimes I can't believe how busy they are.

SANDY: I find they can usually make time. Two-love. (*he serves*) Hurrr (*BONK*).

PHILIP: Actually we're lucky really, (*ball hits wall BONK*) more time to . . .

(PHILIP *hits ball BONK.*)

PHILIP: . . . forge that career . . . (*ball hits wall BONK*) . . . dream those dreams.

(SANDY *hits ball BONK.*)

PHILIP: Sir Chiffley gave us . . . (*ball hits wall BONK*) . . . a dream today . . .

(SANDY *hits ball very hard BONK. Almost immediately it hits wall BONK.* PHILIP *lunges, misses, we hear it hit side wall BONK,* PHILIP *lunges feebly as ball hits three other walls BONK BONK BONK. Finally it goes Dibble Dibble.*)

PHILIP: You see Sandy, that was all over the place.

SANDY: Three-love.

PHILIP: I don't blame you for being distracted. What an inspiration the old man is. Just imagine it Sandy, aeroplanes were Pot Noodles once, and artificial limbs. Hang on to that, it'll see you through when the bulls turn into bears and some secretary's put herbal tea in the Kenco. By crikey, it'd be a pretty strange fellow who could get lonely doing the sort of big, important job we do. Quite frankly I don't have *time* to get lonely.

SANDY: It's three-love. Are you ready . . .

PHILIP: No, bugger it! We've got work to do! (*slap on back, walks off*) Come on soldier, bugger your introspection, if you want to be a philosopher, get a job with Channel Four. We've got arses to kick. So we'll call it a draw, eh?

SCENE THREE

Sir Chiffley's office, as in scene one. It is a month later, it would be nice if a plant or two had flowered.
The CHIEF *and* MISS HODGES.

CHIEF (*perhaps just the slightest hint of adjusting tie*): Thank you Miss Hodges, that was beautifully done. I don't think I've ever known a secretary who could handle a ledger quite like you can.

MISS HODGES: It's kind of you to say so Sir Chiffley.

CHIEF: And such a very heavy one.

MISS HODGES: I'm glad of the exercise Sir.

CHIEF: Do you think it's worth going through it again?

MISS HODGES: Well Sir, you had scheduled a brainstorming session . . .

CHIEF (*glancing at watch*): What? good lord yes, that excited memo from young Philip . . . Is he here?

MISS HODGES: He's outside Sir.

CHIEF: Well send him in girl, send him in.

MISS HODGES: Certainly Sir Chiffley.

(*She exits.* SIR CHIFFLEY *pats the ledger.* PHILIP *enters.*)

PHILIP (*into phone*): Hold all calls.

CHIEF: Sorry to keep you waiting Philip, but I've been considering your memo and I must say it confused me slightly. You say here (*referring to memo*) you've grabbed the challenge by the balls and sunk your teeth into it. Does this mean you have an idea?

PHILIP: Chief, my metaphorical balls are so lacerated you'd think I had a hypothetical crocodile in my trousers. As you know, it's been a few months since you outlined the Pot Noodle brief and I don't mind admitting that those few months have been about as fertile as a dead eunuch.

CHIEF: But no longer.

PHILIP: I think not Sir. You're probably aware that we recently acquired the Associated London Press . . .

CHIEF (*thoughtfully*): Publishing . . . Publishing . . . Yes, good, I'm interested. Not desperately original of course, been done before, but so has bending over a roll-top desk and getting your secretary to beat you on the bottom with a really heavy ledger, and I certainly don't let that stop me.

PHILIP: And why should you.

CHIEF: Associated London is a perfectly decent group of newspapers. All we have to do is turn them into viscous, semi-pornographic, right wing toilet paper and we'll make a mint. Of course Rupert Murdoch will sue us for conceptual plagiarism but it's all good publicity . . .

PHILIP: Uhm, actually Chief, I'm targeting something a little more specific here . . .

CHIEF: I see, well let's have it then lad.

PHILIP: Well Sir, I was checking out the titles we'd acquired, looking for a decent male, adult-interest magazine . . . They have some bloody interesting articles about vintage sports cars in those male, adult-interest magazines you know.

CHIEF: Of course they do and there's nothing dirty or shameful in that.

PHILIP: I suppose I was trying to get my mind off noodles . . . but no go I'm afraid. (*pacing*) I was restless, fretful, I could feel it, I could smell it . . .

CHIEF (*slightly doubtful*): Now then Philip, I'm confused, are we still talking about your idea here? Or have we moved onto male, adult-interest magazines?

PHILIP: Still the idea Chief . . . I knew it was close . . . I'd seen something in one of the papers, but I couldn't recall . . . The little Vodaphone I keep in the back of my head was trying to dial me, but I guess my brain must have been in a meeting . . . . . . Then suddenly . . .

CHIEF: Your brain took the call!

PHILIP: Exactly! The paper I'd been trying to remember was a magazine for hayfever sufferers. (*producing mag*) *The People's Hayfever Listener Examiner Gazette Magazine — Phlegm.* (*hands it over*) Or to put it another way; a Pot Noodle. It says here Chief, and get this . . . they have just invented a machine which is guaranteed to suck in pollen-infested air, extract the pollen, and blow the air out again!!

CHIEF (*after pause*): Well frankly Philip I'm a little disappointed. This is a very junior stuff. Of course we can purchase the patent on this machine if you wish, put the price through the roof. I have no objection to milking a few snot noses.

PHILIP: Hmm, yes but . . .

CHIEF (*the light of enthusiasm*): If I am under any moral obligation to offer a bunch of streamy-eyed sneeze merchants an easy ride, then I am unaware of it.

PHILIP: I was . . .

CHIEF: No dew-drop-hanging free-loader chewing on a mouthful of mucus need expect the feather bed treatment from Lockheart Holdings.

PHILIP: I should say not but . . .

CHIEF: Yes, certainly, go ahead, nail those phlegm-heads to the wall and empty their pockets. If they want pollen-free air, make 'em pay. But really Philip, your secretary should be doing this sort of thing for you.

PHILIP: Chief hear me out! It says here that the machine takes the oxygen from the air, cleans it, and stores it ready for when Cyril Snotnose feels a tickle coming on, when he can give himself a blast of pure, cool oxygen . . .

CHIEF: Stores oxygen? What, like a scuba tank?

PHILIP (*very excited*): Yes but more so . . . the ad says it incorporates a revolutionary compression process which allows considerable quantities of oxygcn to be extracted from the air, and stored for when the sufferer needs to flood the environment with pure nose-fodder.

CHIEF (*still doubtful*): We-ell, interesting concept, I suppose . . . could sell well to marine research, it might even perhaps have some applications in space, but I really don't see . . .

PHILIP (*very excited*): Chief think bigger, think stunningly big, think first-class cabin baggage allowance. What I am talking about here is *designer air*!!!

CHIEF (*after a huge pause*): My God, it's enormous.

PHILIP: I've done some research in sister fields Sir. Water for instance, you can have no concept how big the ponce water market is, and after all, when you come down to it what *is* Perrier? A multi-million pound industry, selling people stuff that falls out of the sky. The French must be absolutely pissing themselves, that's probably what gives the stuff its acrid taste.

CHIEF (*beginning to get excited too*): My dear boy, I think you may have stumbled on something absolutely colossal here, talk me through your thinking so far.

PHILIP: Picture our target consumer right? I had graphics knock me together some visual backup. (*He has visual aids, computer graphics etc. He pieces together or somehow produces a full-size cut-out of a yuppie with a briefcase*) His career is in ascendant mode, his other car really *is* a Porsche. He wants the very best and he intends to get it.

CHIEF: I like him already.

PHILIP: He has a home gym that looks like an iron-lung factory. His yogurt is so alive it shuts the fridge door for him. His muesli is coarse enough to prize open the buttocks of a concrete elephant and his chickens are so free-range he meets them for drinks at his club. And what is he breathing? What is he breathing Chief?

CHIEF: You tell me Philip, you've done the research.

PHILIP: Bus drivers' farts!! That's what he's breathing. He is breathing the same stuff that people in the North are burping their Vimto into. Have you any idea of the cocktail of natural fumes a dog emits when it's on heat? . . .

CHIEF: Pretty gruesome I should imagine.

PHILIP: There are guys out there pulling down *six figure incomes* being forced to breathe that stuff! Something has to be done.

CHIEF (*hitting intercom*): Hold all calls please Miss Hodges and alert security if you'd be so kind, we have a potential Pot Noodle in the building . . . Carry on Philip.

PHILIP: Picture it Chief. You have two wine bars OK? Both are so crowded it takes three days to get a drink. Both have got girls slooshing the plonk with legs sufficiently frisky to revitalize the British motor industry. Both have got a large blackboard that says something indecipherable about game pie . . . But get this, only *one* is offering pure, sparkling, guaranteed filtered, cleansed and mineral-enriched *private* air. Now which hostelry do you think our free-wheeling trouble-shooter who wants the *best* is going to patronize?

CHIEF: Philip, this one, if I might be forgiven some exuberance, is a stallion's stiffy.

PHILIP: It's a whale's whopper.

CHIEF: It's an elephant's appendage.

PHILIP: It's a dinosaur's dong.

CHIEF: It's the giant's giblets. How do we go about acquiring the thing?

PHILIP: Chief, I'm way, way ahead of you. You're still training for 1992 in Barcelona, I'm on my way to Manchester for '96. I have bought up the patent in perpetuity. I also took the liberty of indoctrinating one or two junior top-level executives into the project. (*hits intercom*) Sandy, bring in 'Suck and Blow'.

CHIEF: I like it.

(SANDY *enters with the machine.*)

PHILIP: I suggest that for this demonstration we implement a complete security shut down . . . windows, doors, intercom . . . this thing could be bigger than food.

CHIEF: And food is very big. Activate the shut down Philip.

PHILIP: Sandy, get your butt on it for Chrissakes.

SANDY (*not really enjoying being addressed in this manner*): You got it Philip.

(SANDY *hits a button, huge steel screens descend in front of each window and door etc.*)

PHILIP (*bustling round machine, turning on lights and moving bits*): Now then the chemical reaction which extracts the oxygen is similar in many ways to photosynthesis; it creates gaseous carbon compounds which compensate for the loss of the oxygen in the atmos, so there shouldn't be a pressure drop. But watch out all the same.

SANDY: Pressure doesn't worry me Philip, I am a walking area of high pressure. When I go outside, the weather changes.

CHIEF: I like this young fellow Philip.

PHILIP: My top man Sir, believe me, he's being groomed.

SANDY: If people get too close to me their ears start bleeding.

PHILIP: Yes all right Sandy, let's hit Barry button. (*he presses a button, the machine begins to whirr and hum and flash, steam comes out of it, and a small balloon begins to inflate*) The oxygen is now being extracted Chief, in a few minutes it will all be inside the machine.

SANDY: Uhm Philip . . .

PHILIP: Later Sandy.

SANDY: No really Philip . . .

PHILIP: Not now Sandy.

SANDY: It's just that, if the machine is extracting all the oxygen from the atmosphere, what are we going to breathe?

CHIEF: Good point young fellow.

PHILIP: I encourage all our people to come up with good points Chief.

CHIEF: Good. Are you grooming him?

PHILIP: Like he was a horse Sir.

SANDY: I'm not sure it's working actually, nothing very much seems to be happening (*his knees buckle*).

PHILIP: Get up Sandy, stop playing the giddy ass. (*he collapses*) Sorry Sir, ruck in the carpet.

CHIEF (*gripping desk unsteadily*): What the devil is going on!

SANDY (*pulling himself up unsteadily*): I think it's the machine Sir, we don't notice we're suffocating because the replacement elements fool the lungs into believing that they are breathing normally.

PHILIP (*crawling to feet*): Sandy, are you trying to say that we have stupid lungs because, if so, I take a pretty dim view . . .

CHIEF: I'm getting dizzy, somebody open a window or I shall sack the lot of you!!

(*All very wobbly and faint.*)

PHILIP (*trying to pull up metal screen*): They're all on the security timer Sir! . . .

SANDY: I'll call Miss Hodges . . . (*he moves to the intercom*) hallo . . . hallo . . . She can't hear me, the damn thing's on security shut-off too . . . !

PHILIP: Techno let-down. Try upping the volume on your natural communication system.

SANDY: What?

PHILIP: Shout.

SANDY (*squeaking*): Help . . . help . . . I'm not sure I can Philip . . .

CHIEF (*struggling to get the words out*): If anyone can think of something sensible they will be making a most advantageous career move . . .

(*The machine is now grunting and shaking. The balloon is full.*)

SANDY: Well it's just a thought, but we pressed the button marked 'suck'; maybe we should press the one marked 'blow' . . .

PHILIP (*lying prostrate on his back staring upwards, says faintly*): I was wondering how long it would take you to notice that Sandy. Well done, memo me to intensify your grooming process . . .

(SANDY *staggers to button, the whirring changes. The balloon quickly deflates. Almost instantly they all go* 'AAAAAAH' *with relief.*)

PHILIP: Obviously the instruction manual will have to be very clear on certain points.

(*Blackout.*)

SCENE FOUR

The office of 'Image Control', a top advertising agency.
Total cool, designer work place, big glossy blow-up photos
taken from previous campaigns.
KIRSTEN CARLTON, *a top ad lady.*

KIRSTEN (*on phone*): No dammit Anton, I can't see
you! This is a major pitch for me, Lockheart are
launching an entirely new product and I want the
bloody account . . . . . . Listen if you can't handle
sleeping with someone in a higher income bracket
I'll bike you round a bloody bimbo! Don't bother
to call! (*phone down, hits intercom*) Graham darling,
send in the gentlemen from Lockheart.

(*Enter* PHILIP *and* SANDY . . .)

PHILIP: Kirsten, at long last, I'm Philip, this is my
top man Sandy . . . I can call you Kirsten? You
give such good fax I feel I almost know you,
anyway formalities are totally inefficient.
Whoever said 'manners cost nothing' never had
to play hard ball across eight time zones with the
Tokyo stock exchange.

SANDY: Those guys are tough.

PHILIP: *Terry* tough! By the time you've said
'greetings honourable colleagues' they've bought

your company, miniaturized your lawn mower and eaten your goldfish.

KIRSTEN: Phil, Sand, let me tell you something about me. People tend to address me in one of two ways – it's either 'Kirsten', or 'that tough bitch', you can have it whichever, whichways, whatever way you want it.

PHILIP (*laughing*): I think we're going to get along just fine Kirsty.

KIRSTEN: When you come to Image Control, you come to the best. The media is a minefield of no-talent, sad-act companies whose address is a portable fax machine on the back seat of a Mini Metro.

PHILIP: Exactly.

KIRSTEN: You do *not* require some member-munching mincer with a Design Centre security laminate on his tit . . . (PHILIP *grunts with exasperated recognition*) a Marks and Spencer crudité dip in the saddle bag of his ten-speed racer (*again* PHILIP *understands*) and an ad concept featuring a basking iguana, an enigmatic male model and no mention whatsoever of the actual product because that would be naff.

PHILIP: God, you've met them too?

KIRSTEN: You've come to us because we empty shelves.

PHILIP: That's what the word is on the streets. I play squash with a guy from Imperial Biscuits who says you brought the Jammy Dodger back from the *dead*.

KIRSTEN: I had a small, chemically produced biscuit with a blob of red sticky stuff in the middle of it and my cute little ass was on the *line*. Imperial had given me a *donger* of a budget to push the Jammy Dodger up market, get it out of the tuck shop and into the executive dining room.

PHILIP: It was inspired, I'll never forget it, Penelope Keith pushing the wafer mints away . . . (*plummy voice*) 'Pass a Dodger, Roger.'

SANDY: Brilliant casting, Nigel Havers as Roger was just *so* stylish.

KIRSTEN: Disappointing in bed, surprisingly.

PHILIP: Hmm, yes, well anyway . . . Sandy, I believe you've accessed Kirsty on the relevant base-line information and she's Suck and Blow compatible.

KIRSTEN (*gathering her visual aids together*): Sandy's good Phil, very good.

PHILIP: Believe me he's being groomed. Now then Kirsty I'm not going to pussyfoot around here, I respect you too much and know you have no time for feet in your pussy so tell me, how do you feel about Suck and Blow?

KIRSTEN: Suck and Blow is the most exciting product I've encountered since the Pot Noodle.

PHILIP: Did you hear that Sandy? Rendezvous with destiny or what! This lady worked on the Pot Noodle!

KIRSTEN: My first job . . . 'Put on the kettle, Gretel.'

SANDY: 'Fill my pot, Dot.'

KIRSTEN (*touched*): You remember it.

PHILIP: I feel *very* good about this project, let's have *lunch*!

SANDY: Uhm, perhaps we should ask Kirsten if she's had any time to come up with some ideas yet?

PHILIP: Oh come on Sandy! You've only just accessed here.

KIRSTEN: I like to work fast Phil, I toyed for a while with 'share my air, Claire' but I think it's time to go radical . . . Let me run this byline past you . . . 'Other people's air, it'll get right up your nose.'

(*Short pause, they are thrilled.*)

SANDY: It's . . . brilliant! quite brilliant!

PHILIP: There's a rare and savage beauty to your copy Kirsty.

KIRSTEN (*briskly assembling story boards, presentation portfolios etc*): I'd want to use the fellow who does the Creamy Churn Dairy Spread voice-overs, he turned round their whole campaign with that quiet, sinister way he has . . .

(*Hits a button, we hear a tape . . . . . .*)

TAPE: '*Half* the calories of butter or margarine, but *all* the buttery taste . . .'

PHILIP (*excited*): I buy the damn stuff myself! . . . (*correcting himself*) I mean it always seems to be in the fridge . . . I've got this absolute treasure, I'd probably look totally *Biafran* without her.

KIRSTEN (*hands over designer folder*): You'll find the text on blue . . . We saturate local radio for a fortnight, classic rock and current affairs stations only of course – not a lot of point pitching to some twelve-year-old heavy metal fan whose testicles are still somewhere in the region of his armpits.

PHILIP: With you on that. What about the Telly?

KIRSTEN: I've been thinking hard about television . . . Let's try a little word association game Philip, just for the fun of it, throw me back your instant reactions OK . . . Class.

PHILIP (*instant list*): Bogart, Chivas Regal, Sergeant Pepper, Harley Davidson, Johann Amadeus Bach, mist on a moonlit lake, friendship.

KIRSTEN: You missed something out Philip.

PHILIP: I did?

KIRSTEN: Sandy?

SANDY: Suck and Blow?

KIRSTEN: Exactly.

PHILIP (*short pause, slightly miffed*): Hmm, yes well, I rather thought that went without saying.

KIRSTEN: Nothing goes without saying in advertising Philip, think of Coca Cola. We all *know* it adds life and is the real thing, we don't need reminding that it unites the world, and you can't beat the feeling . . .

SANDY: It really is an incredibly now beverage.

KIRSTEN: Exactly, but if their agency had made the mistake of imagining those things went without saying, we'd be still under the illusion that Coke was just a sweet, sticky drink that can completely dissolve a tooth inside twenty-two hours.

PHILIP: I hope you're listening to all this Sandy. Because you're interjecting on a grade 'A' marketing seminar.

KIRSTEN: OK let's move onto the actual TV time slots. I'm thinking of a sophisticated restaurant scenario here, we're talking real . . .

PHILIP: Class?

KIRSTEN: Exactly.

PHILIP: Wine glasses the size of buckets . . .

(*Plenty of movement, they act it out.*)

KIRSTEN: Only three items on the menu . . .

PHILIP: Portions so small you think you've got a dirty plate and it turns out to be your *main course* . . . (*getting excited*) a hundred and fifty pounds for a splash of raspberry sauce with a squiggly vanilla line through the middle . . . We are talking the very *best* in executive dining.

KIRSTEN: Fine, so you have the venue . . . close-up on two young executive lovers having pre-sex dinner. (*she makes a lens of her fingers, as directors are wont to do*) They are a class act. She is one *heck* of a lady, essentially romantic, but romantic on *her* terms. She has a body that says 'screw me', but watch out because in business hours she'll screw *you*, and screw you to the *wall*. We're looking at a sort of young Meryl Streep with shades of Sigourney Weaver, Jodie Foster, Cher and Sylvester Stallone.

PHILIP: I *like* this lady. What about the guy?

KIRSTEN: Let's just say that our high-class chick is thinking about giving up everything to have his children.

PHILIP: I hope he realizes the kind of levels he's lucked out at.

KIRSTEN: He does, he's one heck of a guy . . . Sandy, you read 'man in restaurant'; I'll read 'sexy girl' . . .

(KIRSTEN *gives him a designer folder.*)

PHILIP: Uhm, hang on, uhm . . . don't you think it would be better if I read 'man in restaurant'? Just a thought.

KIRSTEN: OK you get the part, try it very Michael Douglas. (*she sits at a convenient table, and acts*) . . . 'So darling, next stop the Tokyo posting.'

PHILIP: Right, OK, here goes . . . (*acting*) 'I'm afraid not darling, they've given Tokyo to Simon.'

KIRSTEN (*acting*): 'But you're by far the best man . . .'

PHILIP (*acting*): 'I'm afraid you're going to miss out on all the perks. The magnificent access to Far Eastern shopping facilities, the gorgeous little Sushi bars, the Samurai servants . . .'

KIRSTEN (*acting*): 'Such a shame you didn't get it.'

PHILIP (*acting*): 'Oh I got it all right, I just didn't take it. The office doesn't have Suck and Blow.'

KIRSTEN: And then the voice-over comes in, imagine the man from the Dairy Spread commercials . . . (*hitting tape recording*)

TAPE: 'Remember, a man prepared to breathe second-rate air will probably be prepared to deliver second-rate product. If your people deserve it, fit Suck and Blow.'

PHILIP (*thrilled*): But this is wonderful, I mean absolutely Barry brilliant! Just totally and utterly Barry!

KIRSTEN: It has class Philip.

PHILIP: It has more class than a *Sunday Times* Wine Club special-selection case.

KIRSTEN (*more groovy designer folders*): Item Two uses a similar couple, in a power seduction situation. It's his flat and the lady is hot right? The coffee and Armagnac are all through and she's just about ready to climb aboard and rut her horny little ass off. She just wants to bang her gorgeous, muscly, workaholic, over-achieving boyfriend till his dick falls off.

PHILIP: Ha ha, believe me, I've been that guy.

KIRSTEN: Then you'd better read it again.

(*She slaps another groovy designer folder across at him.*)

PHILIP: Sorry Sandy, perks of seniority . . .

KIRSTEN (*acting*): 'Mmm, lovely coffee . . . I must say you seem to have everything in your beautiful apartment . . . the best food . . . the best wine . . . Only the best of everything, I like that in a man.'

PHILIP (*acting*): 'There's a pool on the roof, I thought we might swim a little later . . .' (*aside to* SANDY) This is *superb*!

KIRSTEN (*acting*): 'As long as it's secluded . . . I don't have a swim-suit. (*she sniffs*) Is something burning? . . . Apart from me that is.'

PHILIP (*aside to* SANDY): I can't *believe* this stuff, it's just *so* believable . . . (*acting*) 'Ha ha, that's the caviar and truffle soufflé ruined.'

KIRSTEN (*acting*): 'Never mind, I'm not hungry – for food, and the Suck and Blow will soon clear the air.'

PHILIP (*acting embarrassed*): 'Uhm . . . hmm . . . yes . . . I'll just open a window shall I?'

KIRSTEN (*acting suddenly cold*): 'Is that the time? I really must be going.' (*hitting tape recording*)

TAPE: 'If you haven't got a Suck and Blow, you haven't got anything at all.'

PHILIP (*very excited*): Kirsten, I don't know what to say. It's quite simply utterly stunning, it could not be more quite simply utterly stunning if you'd written it on a sledge-hammer and bashed young Sandy here over the head with it. Class, you said? This campaign has more class than the *Royal Family*!

KIRSTEN: If you can sell the product into the shops I anticipate commencing a saturation sweep within a matter of weeks. We should be picking up our first major advertising industry awards soon after that.

SANDY: It's a magnificent campaign, we'll sweep the board.

PHILIP: A campaign's no use at all without product outreach. Come along Sandy my son, we've production targets to reach. Check you later Kirsty.

KIRSTEN: You can always get me on the portable.

(*They go,* KIRSTEN *begins to assemble her stuff.* PHILIP *returns alone.*)

PHILIP (*sincere tone*): Kirsten I am a busy man, I did not arrive at where I am today by beating myself with a bush, so I'll put it bluntly. I'm a plain and simple man with plain and simple tastes and I like to see a woman who is both. Can we do dinner?

KIRSTEN: Why not, that would be lovely.

PHILIP: That's OK, no hassle, forget it, I respect a woman who is busy . . . What!

(*Blackout. During the darkness we hear a Capital Radio ad break with a fake Suck and Blow ad in the middle.*)

DJ: And we'll be back with the Capital weather, news of the Help a London Child appeal and of course lots more music, after this . . .

(*Two or three real ads, followed by . . .*)

MUM'S VOICE: Well Jenny, that's the floor done, I've cleaned the house from top to bottom, everything's sparkling and clean for your birthday party.

LITTLE JENNY'S VOICE: No it isn't Mummy.

MUM'S VOICE (*laughing indulgently*): All right Jenny, what have I missed?

JENNY: All the lead, the carbon, the nicotine, the dried dead skin cells, the human methane, oh lots and lots of horrid poisonous muck!

MUM: Well I can't see any of that dear.

JENNY: You can't see it Mummy, but it's there and I'm going to have the dirtiest, most unhealthy birthday party in my class.

VOICE OVER: Doesn't your child deserve the benefits of Suck and Blow . . . ? Other people's air: it'll get right up your nose.

SCENE FIVE

Front of stage, PHILIP *and* CHIEF *wander on with towels wrapped round waists, dripping, wet and sudsy.*

CHIEF (*puffing on huge cigar*): So young fellow, your first dip in the top nobs' Jacuzzi whirlpool bath. I'm sure your telephone will be fine when it's dried out a bit.

PHILIP: It's a legal problem now Chief. When I purchase hardware purporting to be executive level equipment I simply *presume* that it's whirlpool bath compatible. Surely that *has* to be the bottom line.

CHIEF (*taking a robe from an imaginary servant*): Thank you, that will be all . . . (*to* PHILIP) Absolutely first-class steam-room attendant. Totally respectful. It's not often you get respected as well as that these days is it Philip? Respect like that is a rare and precious thing.

PHILIP: Oh no question, the guy gave really terrific respect. Respect-wise, he's a senior talent, a genuine first-division respecter.

CHIEF: One of the little perks of being at the top Philip, is being respected as well as that.

Respected by people who really *know* how to respect. You're going to find yourself on the receiving end of that quality of respect more and more often Philip.

PHILIP: Sounds like pretty heady wine Chief.

CHIEF: Well, I think you know that you've earned it. You've masterminded a Pot Noodle of quite simply colossal proportions. Suck and Blow is the marketing phenomenon of the decade.

PHILIP: Yes, and even more satisfying than the money Chief is that we've improved the quality of people's lives.

CHIEF: Yes, well of course you're right, the social contribution we're making is nice too . . .

(*There are a couple of benches for massage.* CHIEF *addresses an invisible masseur.*)

Just oil me up and calm me down would you, thank you so much . . . (*to another imaginary attendant*) It's my young friend here's first time so loosen him up a bit eh? untie the old muscular knots and bash him into shape, splendid. . . . (*as they get on the benches*) You'll enjoy this Philip, nothing like a massage to relax you after an executive steam.

PHILIP: Yes, I once had a massage in Bangkok, terrific. (*getting on the other bench, discreetly to the imaginary servant*) Just the straight stuff OK? don't bother with the gentleman's executive relief or the lollipop game . . . Mmm, oh yes, most relaxing. (*trying to imply total relaxation and enjoyment*) Oh, oh oh oh *yes*, mmm, that's terrific mm mmm . . . (*he screams*) Ahh!

(*He flings his legs apart . . . i.e. as if the imaginary masseur was pulling him violently.*)

CHIEF (*comfortably immobile with cigar*): Don't worry, he's just breaking down the tissue tension to help you relax.

PHILIP: Fantastic . . . . . . Ahhh!! (*he arches his back violently, speaks with difficulty*) . . . He's a really terrific relaxer . . . . . . Huhhh!! (*he slams his back down and raises his legs straight in the air, all his weight on his shoulders*) Uhhh!!

CHIEF (*still puffing on cigar*): To the victor the spoils Philip, if anyone deserves a moment's relaxation you do.

PHILIP (*straining*): Major compliment received and appreciated Chief. Ahhh!!

(*He flings his legs all the way over so that his toes are on the bench behind his head, he is completely doubled up.*)

CHIEF: People are choosing to purchase Suck and Blow ahead of CD players, microwaves. We penetrate lower income brackets daily. That's what I admire about you Philip, you're flexible.

PHILIP (*straining*): I like to think so Chief . . . . . . Aaaahh!!

(*He does a full backward roll, coming up on his knees. He immediately slams himself face down on the bench.*)

CHIEF: You bend with the marketing wind . . .

PHILIP: I certainly hope so Chief . . . . . Huurrrr!!
(*face down, he lifts chest and knees from bench in a banana shape, balanced on pelvis, then slams down*)
Huurrrr!!

(*He does this a number of times while* CHIEF *carries on*.)

CHIEF: You turn with the trends, you're malleable Philip.

PHILIP (*throwing himself into a headstand*): Chief, I'm just a cog, just a part of the company machine, but I love the company, and when it comes to shifting company product I swear I'm ready to slap my balls right on the line, again and again and again.

CHIEF: I'm sure Abdullah would be quite happy to do that for you . . .

PHILIP (*panicked*): No!! . . . . . . I'd hate to trouble him.

CHIEF: Then perhaps another steam?

PHILIP (*very relieved*): I'd love one Chief.

CHIEF: All right Abdullah, that will do . . . (PHILIP *collapses as if he has been being held up by the feet and has just been dropped,* CHIEF *gets up*) Yes I'm delighted Philip. Why even here in the gym, even through the steam it's clear as crystal, one hundred per cent sterilized, pure, private air.

PHILIP: With a hint of damp pine on a dewy morning if I'm not mistaken.

CHIEF: Let me tell you Philip, I don't miss the reek of stale truss at all. It's a pleasure to draw breath.

As indeed it is in any decent establishment in London these days. (*he walks across and through the steam we see a Suck and Blow machine lurking in the corner, he slaps it appreciatively*) I salute you. And of course your splendid team. I've been delighted with the advertising campaign, that young girl is a marvel. Terribly firm, I like that. It's frisky.

PHILIP: Kirsten is quite literally the best, Chief. That little lady with the cute little ass could get the Pope to sanction condom machines in confession boxes.

CHIEF (*wry*): Am I to presume, Philip, that your fancy is taken?

PHILIP: It's difficult not to be attracted to total excellence Chief.

CHIEF: I don't normally condone liaisons with contracted employees Philip. It blurs future negotiations. If you are thinking of getting involved, I beg you to ask yourself the question, could you marry her and sack her on the same day?

PHILIP: I think partners who can't sack each other don't have much of a relationship, do you Chief?

CHIEF: Well all right then. But steady laddie. Clever women take some handling. A beautiful tradesman's entrance takes the eye, then a keen mind picks the pocket.

PHILIP: Well Chief, I have to say that I see it differently. There's no room in my life for some clueless popsy with a cordon bleu cookery diploma, norkas like melons and a brain like a

grape. If that makes me a feminist then I make
no apologies, but I'm sorry.

CHIEF: I suppose a lot of you young fellows are
feminines these days. Personally, I'm still a bit of
an old sexy myself and I don't mind admitting it.

PHILIP: Different generations Chief, different lifestyle requirements. If I want an attractive cocktail
shaker I'll win the corporate squash tournament
and get awarded one with my name engraved on
it.

CHIEF: It's an attitude I can only admire Philip.
(*jolly, a bit laddish*) Well as the saying goes, faint
heart never got serviced in a variety of interesting
positions and locations so I suggest you stop
lolling about, pull on your shreddies and get
courting.

PHILIP: Reading you Chief.

(*He gets up, the steam has cleared. He begins to dress,
perhaps there is a small chest-high screen, or little block
of lockers to do it behind, or else he just does it under a
towel.*)

CHIEF: So what's your first move, eh? Get her alone
in the conservatory and slip her a box of choccies
with an antique French dildo nestling in the
second layer?

PHILIP: If only.

CHIEF: Too subtle you think?

PHILIP: Oh no it's not that, it's just that . . . well to
tell you the truth I'm not awfully good when it
comes to talking to totty. Oh I'm all right with

business but when it comes to anything remotely gropey, I'm a clam. I took Kirsten to dinner only last week, and we talked about nothing but sucking and blowing all evening . . . Ended up discussing the staff, she nearly managed to poach Sandy off me, clever bitch . . . I just could not bring myself to nudge the situation onto more intimate lines.

CHIEF: Like so many great men before you, a daunting figure of power and confidence in battle, but a gawking, shuffling boy in matters fruity eh?

PHILIP: That's me Chief. It's a hell of a handicap when you're trying to unload your cherry, I can tell you Sir. I got so tongue-tied on any subject but work that she actually mentioned it. Said I was hopeless at small talk, said any girl interested in me would probably have to pitch in and damn well ask me herself.

CHIEF: Well whatever the situation is *vis à vis* cherry disposal Philip, you mustn't let it distract you from the main task, and that is the continued success of Suck and Blow (*again he slaps the machine*). We must be very careful, we're in danger of becoming victims of that very success. The Japanese are already in. It hasn't taken those clever fellows long to strip down a sucker and wrest from it its secret.

PHILIP (*bitterly*): And as far as Mr Suzuki-Mitsubushi-the-war-was-nothing-to-do-with-me-squire is concerned we can stuff our patents-pending right up our polite English bum holes. These people

just don't play fair Chief. Look at what they did
to the British motor industry! Deliberately and
maliciously destroying it by making better cars.
They have a four and a half *million* letter
alphabet and they still can't spell the word
'decency'.

CHIEF: Well you started this Philip, it is your job to
keep us ahead. I'm giving you *full* responsibility, I
want you to live, sleep and *breathe* 'air'.

PHILIP: It will be the deepest of privileges Chief.
After all, Suck and Blow isn't just about money.
Hell, let the Japs have a piece. We are building
the future here, making a better, healthier,
cleaner world for our children . . .

CHIEF: Children eh? I must say this clever little lady
with the attractive cul-de-sac certainly seems to
have made an impression.

PHILIP: Well I don't know Chief, call me a total drip
if you like but things just seem to be so bloody
right at the moment; major career upswing,
beautiful girl . . . . . . As long as I can sort out the
old nerves and slip her an offer that is.

CHIEF: You will lad, you will, you can't help being
sensitive. Now have you got my briefs?

PHILIP: No question Chief: live, sleep and *breathe* air.
I'm with you.

CHIEF: No, I meant have you got my briefs? These
aren't mine, (*pair of pants*) they've got a cartoon
representation of a maggot emerging from an
apple on the front, and the words 'girl bait'.

PHILIP: What! . . . . . . good lord, sorry Chief, wasn't
thinking, sorry. (*he is dressed, checks in his trousers*)
Silly Christmas present, keep meaning to chuck
them . . .

CHIEF: Philip, believe me, you're the top coming
man, but I don't think you're quite ready to move
into my underpants yet, eh?

PHILIP: God forbid Chief.

CHIEF: I don't need his help, I give my own orders.
You've got yours, now give me my skidders, bung
on your own, get out there and turn the whole
nation into suckers.

SCENE SIX

KIRSTEN*'s office. New story boards and stuff.*
There is a large shiny Suck and Blow in corner.

PHILIP: I don't believe this Kirsten, why it's not two
months since the Chief told me to live, sleep and
breathe air! There can't be a problem!

KIRSTEN: Philip I don't care what Sir Chiffley said,
I'm telling you, the first surge is over. With the
Japs and the Yanks in, competition is getting
more intense and demand is falling. We have
definitely got a glitch in the gusset.

PHILIP: Hell, bugger.

KIRSTEN: I've got figures to pitch at you that will be
harder to swallow than an Aeroflot breakfast.

PHILIP (*into portable phone*): Hold all calls.

KIRSTEN: Sales-wise, my research teams are
predicting downswing.

PHILIP: Downswing or Plummet swing?

KIRSTEN: The household and domestic market is
dead set to dump faster than an Italian-made
kite.

PHILIP: Are you saying that there is a problem with *the* boom product of the decade?

KIRSTEN: Problem is not a word I like Phil, me and the word 'problem' do not get along. If the word 'problem' were to take me out for the evening I'd be home by nine-thirty and curled up with a good book five minutes later.

PHILIP: Well quite.

KIRSTEN: Nonetheless, production is definitely too high for the current market to absorb. Lockheart have shifted *three million* units in the UK alone, never mind Sony, Westinghouse, K-Tel. Even the Sinclair model is selling and that pumps nitrogen . . . look at this . . .

(*An enormously thick newspaper of seven or eight inches.*)

PHILIP: A copy of last week's *Sunday Times*. Superb article on arms smuggling, terrific graphic of a huge arrow with a gun drawn on it, going from Iraq to a Semtex factory in Czechoslovakia, made it all so clear . . .

KIRSTEN (*taking a thin section from the huge paper*): Take a look at Section 27, part 4, the 'Lifestyle' pull-out is devoted entirely to the second-hand Suck and Blowers. The domestic market is saturated, we need to target much more specifically, there are a thousand areas in which people could be persuaded to expect private air. Doctors' waiting rooms, bus stations, theatres, factories.

PHILIP: So you think with the right marketing you can de-glitch the gusset?

KIRSTEN: With the right marketing you can do anything you want Philip. If we handle this glitch properly, before we know it Lockheart will make you President of the whole air division . . . but it needs the right marketing. (*tiny hint of sauciness*) And of course with the right marketing . . . girl.

PHILIP (*suddenly nervous*): . . . Well, we've . . . uhm, I mean *I've* or rather we've, I've, certainly got that Kirsten. I don't know what Suck and Blow would have done without you.

KIRSTEN: Or me without it. You know Philip, this campaign has been pretty exciting for me . . . in more ways than one.

PHILIP (*tongue-tied*): So. (*his voice breaks into squeak*) How's . . . I'm sorry, (*deep voice*) how's that Kirsten?

KIRSTEN (*a bit sexily*): We-ell, let's just put it this way . . . That there's a certain *horny* chick from Creative Marketing (*touches him teasingly*) who's been working pretty closely with a certain *hot* guy from Lockheart . . . And this certain horny chick reckons this certain hot guy is sort of special, OK? You know, a real *tasty geezer*! Are you with me Phil?

(*More flirty touching.*)

PHILIP: Ah, hmm, yes, uhm . . .

KIRSTEN: What's more I've got a kind of girly suspicion that with the right persuasion he'd rut like a charging elephant and could find a G-spot blindfold with his hands tied behind his back.

PHILIP (*very embarrassed*): Coo, Harry hot in here isn't it? I'll just open a window shall I?

KIRSTEN: Now don't change the subject . . . anyway, better not, the air's been sucked a bit thin out there today . . . (*crosses to him*) But what I want to know, Philip, is do you think I'm right about this *hot hunky* guy . . . ? After all . . . (*touches him again*) you know him much better than I do.

PHILIP: Well I . . . hmmm, yes, elephant you say? God, I don't know . . . perhaps (*hurriedly packing briefcase*) . . . Look, hell Kirsten I've really got to charge, I mean rut, I mean run! Meetings to orgasm, I mean organize. People to sex, see! . . . Anyway, right, bye!

KIRSTEN: You won't forget what I've said will you Philip?

PHILIP: Twelve types of no way, I mean, no way for sure!

(*Blackout. In the darkness we hear* PHILIP *cry out in frustration.*)

PHILIP: Oh Barry Bollocks!!!

(*During the continued blackout we hear the voice of a theatre announcer.*)

ANNOUNCER: Ladies and gentlemen, before we continue with tonight's performance you may like to know that before our next production, which will be Andrew Lloyd Webber's new musical *Aspects of Mussolini*, this theatre will be fitted with Suck and Blow machinery throughout so that all

our patrons may enjoy the safety and the quality
of one hundred per cent filtered private air.
Thank you for your attention.

SCENE SEVEN

SANDY *is walking across stage, with briefcase and portable phone, doing business in the street.*

SANDY: Hallo Gary? Yeah we won the case, Philip is going to sodding *ejaculate*! . . . Yeah the judge ruled parents have the right to switch their kids' schools on air cleanliness grounds, the implications are enormous . . . I really think it's time we started pressing the Home Office on prisons, I mean quite apart from the humanitarian arguments, with minor adjustments it could be a superb way of inputting tear gas . . . (*a ringing*) Oh bugger, hang on Gary . . . (*produces a second phone*) Yo Tony! Just talking to Gary . . . (*into first phone*) Gary, it's Tony . . . (*back to second phone*) Tony, can you hold . . . (*back to first phone*) Yo Gary, I'm back . . . (*another ringing*) Bugger! Hang on Gary . . . (*into second phone*) Hang on Tony . . . (*produces a third phone*) Speaking . . . Great Jurgen, *guten Tag* . . . (*first phone*) Gaz, its Jurgen . . . (*second phone*) Tone, it's Jurgen (*third phone*) . . . Listen Jurgen, I'm just speaking to Gary and Tony . . . (*another ringing*) Bollocks . . . (*first phone*) Hang on Gaz . . . (*second phone*) Hang on Tone . . . (*third phone*) *Eine Minute* Jurgo . . .

(*answers fourth phone*) Yo . . . Geoff thanks for
getting back . . . (*first phone*) Gaz, it's Geoff . . .
(*second phone*) Tone, it's Geoff . . . (*third phone*)
Jurgo, its Geoff . . . (*fourth phone*) Listen Geoff,
you'll have to hold, I'm just talking to Gaz, Tony
and Jurgen . . . (*another ringing*) Heigh ho. (*first
phone*) Gaz, I'm pulling in a lot of favours here
but I'm going to need two ticks' worth of
breathing space . . . (*second phone*) Tone, it's got to
be a peco-sec minimum . . . (*third phone*) *Achtung*
Jurgo, look it's a totally *Donner und Blitzen*
situation over here, I feel like an utter
Schweinhund but you'll have to hold . . . (*fourth
phone*) Geoff, I've got LA in one ear, Frankfurt in
another and the Space Shuttle in a third, be right
back . . . (*he produces fifth phone either from under a
hat or straight out of the Khyber Pass*) Phil! Yeah we
won! The anti-air lobby got a *serious* case of
brewer's droop . . . Phil, give me an eighth of a
tick . . . (*first phone*) Listen Gaz, talk to Tone (*he
holds both phones together in one hand . . . third phone*)
Jurgo? *sprechen Sie mit* Geoff will you? (*two phones
together in other hand . . . fifth phone is now between
knees*) Phil? (*with briefcase under arm he begins to
bunny-hop off whilst talking into fifth phone*) Yeah,
you have to believe it Phil, their dicks were
pointing *south* . . .

(*A sixth ringing as lights go. This time the ringing is
very loud to cover him hopping off.*)

SCENE EIGHT

Lights straight up again. The boardroom. CHIEF, PHILIP, SANDY. *There is champagne as in the first scene. The phone continues to ring from end of previous scene.* SANDY *is demonstrating.*

CHIEF (*interrupting* SANDY, *picks up phone*): Not now Miss Hodges.

SANDY: So as you can see Chief, I'm very excited; what I'm barely suppressing here is blue chip, gilt-edged excitement . . . since Philip and Kirsty bashed out their deep penetration policy . . .

PHILIP (*distracted*): If only . . .

SANDY: Sorry?

PHILIP: Nothing.

SANDY: In the incredibly short time since then, private air has become the bottom line for just about any enclosed space in the country. Sales are soaring steeper than an up bound 747 scraper-hopping out of Hong Kong.

CHIEF: Yes, and I think perhaps a small celebration is in order . . . (*crossing to drinks trolley*) Gentlemen, allow me to propose a toast . . . a toast to Philip, the first President of the entire Lockheart Air Division.

SANDY (*surprised*): Hells bells! Senior career upswing! Well done Philip!

PHILIP (*surprised but a little preoccupied*): President . . . ! Chief I had no idea . . . I don't know what to say.

CHIEF: You seem a trifle underwhelmed my boy.

PHILIP: Oh no way Chief, I mean absolutely thirty-seven types of no way Chief!

CHIEF: Philip, I am Sir Chiffley Lockheart. I have more money than God and I am not a fool, please don't treat me as one. What's on your mind?

PHILIP (*slightly taken aback*): Well I . . .

CHIEF: Come on, out with it, nobody loves a shillier, no more do they a shallier, let us have your thoughts.

PHILIP (*after a moment's hesitation*): Chief, nobody wants to poop on the parade but I pride myself on being a realist, I like to think I give better realism than an omnibus edition of *EastEnders*. Well this is where I get real. Chief, the party's over.

SANDY (*shocked*): What!

CHIEF: You surprise me Philip.

PHILIP: What can I tell you? I am hoovering up stale crisps and trying to get red wine stains out of the shag pile. The party is definitely on its last legs. I

don't like it, my people don't like it, but there you
are. The problem is Sir that the machines store
too much. People are strange fish, the capacity
exists so they fill it . . . they are stockpiling
oxygen.

(PHILIP *hands out reports.*)

CHIEF: I'm aware of that development Philip, kindly
explain the problem. It's not as if the world is
short of oxygen, we'd need literally billions of
machines to noticeably affect the make up of the
atmosphere.

PHILIP: Oh absolutely Sir, in broad terms there is
clearly no problem . . . locally however, the story
can be somewhat different. As you are aware Sir,
when the machines suck in oxygen they create an
equal and opposite amount of carbon
compounds, hence there is no pressure drop.

SANDY: Which has been considered essential right
from the very beginning, no unseasonal winds are
created, the weather remains unaffected.

PHILIP: Hmm yes, unfortunately until a natural
wind blows . . . within the localized environment,
where mass sucking is taking place, there can
develop a bit of a shortfall on breathing
material . . . not for very long, but well, 'not very
long' is actually quite a while in respiratory
terms . . . It's suddenly all got rather serious, in
some areas brief periods have arisen where
strolling for a bus has been a similar experience
to climbing Mount Everest.

SANDY (*looking at report*): Unfortunately, without the
accompanying exhilaration, sense of personal

achievement and potential to capitalize on your name through commercial sponsorship.

CHIEF: I see.

PHILIP: We are beginning to be looking at a potential scenario where grannies could start keeling over in the streets.

SANDY: Chief I have to tell you, that sort of development could be a public relations nightmare.

PHILIP: The same thing's happening abroad. There's a lot of wild talk about massively prohibitive licence fees, possibly even a blanket ban. I very much fear that Suck and Blow is spiralling into Dodo mode.

CHIEF: I see. You're clearly rather depressed about this Philip. What about you Sandy, are you as depressed as Philip?

SANDY: If anything I'm slightly more depressed.

CHIEF: Hmm, I feel terrific.

SANDY (*tiny pause*): I must say I'm perking up.

CHIEF: It seems to me gentlemen, that what we are doing here is forgetting the Moon landings.

PHILIP (*mystified*): Ahhhm, yes Chief, you're right, I did leave the Moon landings out of this particular equation . . . was that terribly wrong of me?

CHIEF: The Moon landings were a financial disaster of horrendous proportions. Twenty billion dollars to achieve two small bags of dust; so much had been hoped of them; so little achieved; it would have been better if they had never even bothered. Until that is, somebody noticed the Velcro.

PHILIP: Velcro, Chief?

CHIEF: Millions of nylon hooks and eyes on fabric strips.

PHILIP: Uhm . . . . . . yes, I know what it is, but . . . ?

CHIEF: Developed for specific uses during the space programme, then somebody decided to stick it on anoraks and turned it into a Pot Noodle. Within fifty years it will have paid for the whole fiasco. Out of evil came forth good. Gentlemen, we must find new ways to use our machinery.

PHILIP: Uhm yes, forgive me Sir, but it's *using* the machines that's the problem. I really am rather concerned that well . . . . . . we might have produced a product that might well . . . . . . kill someone.

SANDY: With all due respect to Philip, if the tobacco industry had taken that kind of line, some of the world's greatest sporting events would never have been sponsored.

CHIEF: No no, I think that Philip has a point, we certainly don't want deaths on our conscience, bad for morale, bad for business. However, a solution presents itself which also opens up a whole new world of commerce and profit.

PHILIP: It does?

CHIEF: It's really very simple . . . We build Super Suckers and Bumper Blowers, far in advance of anything currently available, and undertake to

collect oxygen in under-populated areas. Then
councils who find their atmospheres temporarily
thinned, through, I might add, the actions of
their own citizens, will be in a position to make
up the shortfall by hiring us to pump some back
into the public arena.

SANDY: My God! It's brilliant.

PHILIP: So Chief, you're suggesting that having
made a huge profit from machines by which
people hoard oxygen, we now build bigger
versions of the same machines, in order to make
further profits replacing it.

CHIEF: Exactly.

PHILIP: Look Chief, call me an insanely cautious old
turd if you will; look me in the eye and say 'Phil,
if you drag your feet any further you're going to
be tripping over *tube* trains'; ring my people and
tell them that their boss wouldn't recognize solid
gold if he was surrounded by three quarters of a
million Californians jumping up and down,
waving their pick axes and shouting 'yeeha, we've
struck it', I just feel that there's going to be
objections.

CHIEF: Philip, we didn't create this situation, we only
make the machines. If a problem exists, the
consumer has created it and thank God we live in
a society where the consumer has a right to create
problems.

PHILIP (*still doubtful*): Yes, I see that certainly, it's just
that, well . . . selling air? I see a media backlash,
and frankly, I'm buggered if perhaps they

wouldn't have a point. I mean, everybody owns the air, don't they? We don't really have a right to sell it? Do we? Or what?

CHIEF (*a tiny bit angry*): Yes Philip, and while you're taking your Ph.D. in moral semantics Mr Suzuki is laying down the keel of the first Super Sucker. You're my top man Philip, President of the division and quite frankly I'm surprised . . .

SANDY (*pleased*): Perhaps you're tired Phil. You drive yourself like an insane man.

CHIEF: The air is a natural resource. Like food or coal. Is the grocer or the coal man wrong for selling his wares? And yet people need food and warmth as much as they need air. It seems that a man is to be allowed to put bread on his table, clothes on the backs of his children, buy land upon which they can run and play, and yet he is to be denied the chance to provide fully and properly for his family the most basic human prerequisite of the lot, the wherewithal to breathe. Denied that chance for fear that some hypothetical, free-loading drop-out may find himself momentarily short of breath.

SANDY: Phil, this is more than a business venture, it's a moral crusade!

PHILIP: You're right Sandy . . . sorry Chief, just thinking things through that's all.

CHIEF: I understand my boy . . . A fellow's always a bit soft and loopy when he's in love eh? Any developments on that front yet? Can't have you mooning about for ever.

PHILIP: Well she did say something quite encouraging a month or two back . . . haven't quite got round to acting on it yet.

CHIEF: Ha ha, well you get on with it lad. Got to clear the air my boy. So that we can sell it.

ACT TWO

SCENE ONE

The control room of a huge air supplier, consoles of buttons and flashing lights, computer screens, electronic maps of Britain with different coloured areas and arrows on them that could mean wind direction. If possible the arrows should move and the lights and stuff flash etc. There is celebration bunting hanging about, the Lockheart Logo is very prominent, there is a dais and a ribbon to be cut, a table full of champagne. It is clearly a media opening.

(PHILIP, *in black tie, is alone . . .*)

PHILIP (*nervously rehearsing a speech*): . . . It's just that what you said to me that time at Image Control . . . deeply sensible of enormous honour, yes deeply . . . Oh God, oh God . . . Come *on* Philip, be a man for Christ's sake, she's damn *hot* for you too so just *go* for it!

(*Enter* KIRSTEN *also dressed for launch.*)

KIRSTEN: Go for what Philip?

PHILIP (*confusion*): What? Oh, just all this Kirsty, you've really gone for it, no woman could do more, a truly Herculean effort. Christ, I don't think I've ever *seen* so much champagne and dippy things.

KIRSTEN (*checking things*): Well Philip, I can't deny I'm confident, the Industry awards for the most champagne and dippy things at a launch are next month and I think our only real competition will be the first night of *Aspects of Mussolini*. I was very worried about last week's Channel Four re-re-relaunch but they blew it by switching to Asti Spumante after Michael Grade left.

PHILIP (*looking about*): This launch is terribly important to me Kirsty, it's a hearts and minds launch.

KIRSTEN: Which is why it's so important to get the champagne and dippy things right . . . Top quality bite-sized savoury thingies and plenty of them. (*motions to table*) The times I've heard high-level opinion-formers dismiss an entire product range on the strength of soggy filo pastry.

PHILIP: Well this little lot should guarantee some decent coverage.

KIRSTEN: You can never, never tell . . . you can have the most successful launch of all time, then Princess Di gets out of a low slung sports car, some hack gets a decent shot of her knickers and you'll be lucky if the press find room for you on the sports pages.

PHILIP: It just goes to show 'there ain't no such thing as a free lunch.'

KIRSTEN (*slightly offended*): Well there isn't any call for that kind of comment.

PHILIP (*confused*): What? I mean did I . . . ?

KIRSTEN (*a zealot on her pet subject*): Free lunch is
what keeps the mighty cogs of public relations
turning. Why without free lunch there would be
no more magazines, no more pop records, no
more television programmes, no new estate
agents opened . . .

PHILIP: God, heaven forbid.

KIRSTEN: Free lunch is the universal lubricant . . .
from a tiny, two-person, tax-deductible power
pasta to a six-hundred-head media faceful like
this. Without free food London would stop
moving, we'd be a third world country in a
month.

PHILIP: You're absolutely right Kirsty, sorry . . . A
fellow gets so tied up in his own little area that
it's shamefully easy to forget the quite incredible
amount of dedicated eating that has to go on just
to bring a product before the public.

KIRSTEN: PR and Media *is* the product Philip. As
you say, it's hearts and minds.

PHILIP: Yes, no more so than in this case. Sadly
there are still people who rather resent their
councils having to buy in private air to make the
streets safe. We've got to get people to
understand that pushing private air into the
public arena is the inevitable result of people's
God-given right to own their own air.

KIRSTEN: The press packs are very clear. (*glossy
brochure*) I've had my very best people working on
the buzz words and catch phrases . . . (*flicking
through*) I'm particularly pleased with 'air's fair',

and 'an Englishman's nose is his castle' . . . (*looking at watch*) Christ is that the time! Sir Chiffley will be here any moment, and I haven't checked that the waitresses' little black skirts are short enough . . . (*She makes to leave.*)

PHILIP (*slightly embarrassed, grabbing his moment*): Uhm, hang on a moment Kirsten . . . there was something I wanted to say . . .

KIRSTEN: Better make it quick Phil . . .

PHILIP: What? oh yes, of course . . . well it's just that . . . Oh hell, I'm not much good at this sort of thing . . . I wanted to tell you that you have got the most fantastic . . . most fantastic . . . people . . . No really, you have great . . . people and . . . and well . . . I'd really like to get my hands on them . . .

KIRSTEN: Thanks Philip, I'll memo them.

PHILIP: I'd like to memo them too Kirsten. Yes I would, I'd like to give them a bloody good memo-ing, I mean it . . . and it's not just your . . . . . . people . . . . . . I also love your . . . . . . presentation, you have beautiful presentation . . . . . . You're a very special lady Kirsten . . .

KIRSTEN: What's on your mind Phil, is there a problem?

PHILIP: Problem? a hundred and twelve types of 'no way'! . . . . . . It's just, it's just that well . . . . . . Oh this is ridiculous, I don't need to be embarrassed, after all, I know how *you* feel.

KIRSTEN: You do?

PHILIP: Yes of course I do . . . after what you said in the office that day, about the tasty elephant with G-spots on his geezer . . .

KIRSTEN: Oh . . . . . . you remembered.

PHILIP: Of course I remembered, Kirsty-wirsty. Christ I'm young, Christ I'm romantic, Christ I'm a tasty elephant . . . The world's beautiful and so are we . . . . . . And, I want you to know that it's *all right* . . . . . . I feel the same way.

KIRSTEN: You do?

PHILIP: Yes! isn't that marvellous! It's like it was meant to happen. *You* feel it, *I* feel it . . . we're already a team.

KIRSTEN (*very cold*): I'm sorry Philip, there's no way it will work. Yes all right, I admit what I feel, why shouldn't I? But I had no idea you felt it too, honestly if I'd thought for a moment that we both felt the same way then I would never have started this damn thing.

PHILIP: Christ, you girls don't half make it difficult! Look, pretty speeches aren't normally my line, but I really do think you're one *hell* of a bit of skirt, top-notch totty, senior bint etc. and any *normal* guy would·have to be *blind* not to develop a major *horn* for you.

KIRSTEN: Philip, trying to flatter me isn't going to change anything, if you know how I feel you should understand that.

PHILIP: Of course I know how you feel, I know you're *hot* for the top stallion in the Lockheart stables, and I'm ready and willing to take the jumps with you!!

KIRSTEN: Right that's enough! Just shut up right now! It's disgusting. I had no idea you felt this way, but let me tell you I'm not sharing Sandy with you and if you two are planning some kind of dirty little AC/DC three-up sex game, count me out!

PHILIP: Oh come on baby, why don't you just drop the pretence, drop the inhibitions, drop your pantyhose and let's do it!! . . . . . . Sharing Sandy? What . . . what do you mean?

KIRSTEN: You said you feel the same way I do, well if you fancy Sandy go for it mate but don't expect me along for the ride.

PHILIP: Uhm . . . . . . look, I think there's a chance I may have dropped something of a clanger here . . . That day in your office, when you were bowling hints that there was a hot, hunky guy at Lockheart and you wanted in . . . you were . . . . . . referring to Sandy?

KIRSTEN: Yes, I've liked him since that first day at my office. I thought you knew. I talked about him half the evening that night we went to dinner. I virtually never see him so I was hoping that you might drop a hint in the right direction . . . . . . Hang on . . . . . . Oh *God* this is funny, you didn't . . . . . . you didn't think that I fancied *you*?

PHILIP: Oh no! not at all . . . . . . well yes, sort of . . . . . . anyway, ha ha, senior communication breakdown eh?

KIRSTEN: I should say so. *God* that is *so funny!*

PHILIP: You should have gone through your
people . . . or sent a fax . . .

KIRSTEN: I suppose it would have been simpler. Still
no harm done eh?

PHILIP: No, of course not . . . None whatsoever . . .
You really think it's funny do you?

KIRSTEN: Of course, don't worry about it, I'm not
offended or anything, I just think it's an
incredible joke don't you?

PHILIP: Of course, of course, of course. Ha ha.

(*Fade to black.*)

(*A huge sob is heard. Lights up, it is a little later,* SIR
CHIFFLEY *is at the podium,* PHILIP, *and* SANDY, *all in
dinner jackets, respectfully flank him.*)

CHIEF (*making speech*): . . . Far in advance of any of
our competitors, Lockheart Air Division has
completed this major central distribution co-
ordination master control room . . . When it
comes on line, this facility will be able to access
sufficient oxygen to waft the whole of Greater
London for up to twenty-eight days . . . The air
industry has come of age. At last we have a
secure base from which to serve the public . . .
Now then gentlemen, ladies, I'm sure I've spoken
enough and lunch is waiting.

(*He steps down to polite taped applause. Immediately on
tape the sounds of a crowd eating and chatting start
up.*)

(*Lights up. It is a little later,* SIR CHIFFLEY *is at the podium,* PHILIP, GEOFF *and* SANDY, *all in dinner jackets, respectfully flank him.*)

CHIEF (*making speech*): . . . and so the doctor said 'Big breaths Marjorie' and Marjorie replied 'Yeth doctor and I'm only thixteen' . . . (*after small laugh*) Now, of course there is in fact a very serious point to that story. For without the facilities that Lockheart Air Division can offer, facilities like this Central London Wafter which Lady Olga has so kindly opened for us – a wafter far in advance of anything our competitors are currently providing – without that, no doctor would feel confident in ordering a patient to take 'big breaths'. Rather he would be obliged to say 'tiny pants Marjorie' which, let's face it, quite apart from being totally inadequate on health grounds, would be a completely different joke. So there you are then, I think I've made my point, and now gentlemen, ladies, lunch is waiting.

(*Lights up, the event is over, tables are an empty mess, etc.*
SANDY *and* PHILIP *are with* CHIEF, bow ties a bit undone etc. PHILIP *is slightly pissed.*)

PHILIP: Well Chief, a splendid speech, and a splendid launch in general . . . . . . very inspiring . . . . . . I feel great. I really do.

SANDY: Yes marvellous Chief, gives one a terrific glow. Mind you, we . . .

PHILIP (*rudely interrupting him*): Yes Chief, it's certainly a wonderful facility.

SANDY (*ignoring* PHILIP): We could have done without the press going on and on about how much actual oxygen is getting through to the consumer . . .

CHIEF: I share their concern Sandy, it's the classic problem of over-production. All the franchise holders have been sucking away like a hyperactive Rent boy, and now the UK's been semi sucked out and we're all sitting on huge tanks of compressed oxygen.

SANDY: Everyone's undercutting (*motions to areas flashing on maps*) It's beginning to look like a fullscale price war Sir.

PHILIP (*aside to* SANDY): Yes all right, just pack in the leering innuendo bit OK? You can have her, I don't give a toss. (*back to* CHIEF) It isn't so much the price I'm concerned about Chief, it's more that not enough air is actually being wafted to the breathing public.

CHIEF: Well we can't very well waft it until we've agreed a decent price for it can we? Or what's the point of sucking it in the first place? We just have to get together with the other franchise holders and establish a stable minimum price. Good lord, if a bunch of wops with dishtowels on their heads can establish an oil cartel, I think we should be just about able to set a decent price for a gulp of air.

SANDY: Well I hope you're right Chief, things are very unstable at the moment. We've seen green stamps, air miles, royal crested teaspoons, sherry schooners. It's insane! Do they really want to have to fight a free gift war? That's the kind of war nobody wins.

PHILIP (*waspish*): Oh God, state the obvious why don't you Sandy. Sorry Chief, I think his mind's on *other things*!!

(*Nobody really knows how to react.*)

CHIEF: A free gift war would be a nightmare, we all know very well that free gift wars lead to shooting wars and by heaven I shan't allow hot headedness of that sort to ruin this industry. Look what's happened in France, organized crime, protection rackets. Thank goodness the process leaves the atmosphere non-volatile so, within limits, it is possible to administer an area on a regional basis.

SANDY: Apart, of course, from the wind.

PHILIP (*still waspish*): Yes well we all know *that*.

SANDY: Only two days ago in Hounslow, Essex we're scheduled to top up twelve thousand houses, plus the council is taking delivery for its street wafting obligations. Our boys are two miles out of town in a twelve sucker convoy. What happens . . . the wind.

PHILIP (*unpleasantly imitating* SANDY): 'The wind.'

SANDY (*ignoring him*): Suddenly everyone's jumping for joy and stuffing their sucker tubes out of the window.

PHILIP: Well at least everybody got something to breathe, I mean that's important too isn't it? I mean fair's fair, the wind's the wind after all.

SANDY: Philip, they were getting *free* air, where the hell does that leave us?

CHIEF: No Philip's right, the wind is the wind and I see no reason why we cannot put it to our advantage, most winds are fairly seasonal. It seems to me not an unreasonable idea that we might anticipate the majority of them.

PHILIP (*not understanding*): Ye-es.

CHIEF: And send mobile suckers to the coast in order to harvest the oxygen before the winds sweep inland. That way the basic minimum gulp price will be protected and the legitimate consumer will be protected from cowboys.

PHILIP: Well of course, we have to protect the consumer.

SANDY: The needs of the customer must come first.

PHILIP: I just *said* that Sandy.

SCENE TWO

A TV WEATHER WOMAN *comes on and stands by map with her little cloud and rain stickers. She tries to be jokey in a farty, weedy way.*

WEATHER WOMAN: Well I certainly hope some of you were enjoying the beautiful sunshine we've been experiencing in the South East. I know my roses were pretty pleased to see me . . . I'll tell you what . . . I don't know about talking to plants, but if my roses could talk to me, I expect they'd say uhm . . . 'Where have you been darling, don't see much of you' and 'what about these greenfly?' ha ha. Anyway moving on to tomorrow's weather, well the most exciting thing is some very strong winds coming in over the Bristol Channel. Now these will be fresh in from the Atlantic and so they're likely to be completely full. Really brisk, lovely, oxygen-saturated winds, so why not get the Suck and Blow in the car and go and pick a few breaths up for nothing . . . make a family picnic of it.

    Now a word of warning, there will also be strong gusting in the North West, but please don't get excited, that one's in from Scandinavia, and I'm afraid it will have been well and truly milked by the Swedes. Of course it may have picked up something over the North Sea, but I should leave that one to the professionals if I were you. Personally I'll be sticking with my roses ... ha ha, don't want them whispering about me behind my back. Ha ha ha. Good night.

SCENE THREE

It is KIRSTEN's *flat. She and* SANDY *have just hosted a dinner party. She is at the door seeing out guests who we do not see.*

KIRSTEN: It was lovely to see you Geoff, *Christ* knows when was the last time I got a bit *pissed*. Thanks for the lovely Shiraz by the way, I *love* Australian wine, it always walks away with the blind tastings . . . Anyway it's been absolutely great, see you again *soon* . . . mmm, wonderful, bye . . . . . . bye . . . . . . (*she closes the door and walks back in*) God that bloody bloke can *breathe*!

SANDY: What?

KIRSTEN: I could not *believe* it? Could you believe it? I couldn't. I mean it's not necessary is it? Sitting there like some great vacuum cleaner *sucking* in great gusts of the stuff. The man must have lungs like zeppelins.

SANDY: Seemed perfectly normal to me.

KIRSTEN: I'm sure he could discipline himself to take smaller breaths, I mean it's just *rude*, it's not as if the stuff grows on trees. Next time I think I shall *have* to say something, just a little joke like 'coo mind you don't suck up the sofa'. I mean it is unbelievable don't you think . . . ?

SANDY: Oh come on Kirsten, he's an active bloke, I mean he has to breathe. Anyway, you didn't have to stand with the door open saying goodbye did you.

KIRSTEN: Sandy, may I remind you that this is my bloody house, for which I work bloody hard and if I wish to stand with the bloody door open I shall bloody well do so!

SANDY: I'm just saying that if you're so worried about your air it's not your job to supply the whole street. You could have said goodbye with the door closed you know.

KIRSTEN: Sandy, working in creative marketing may not be quite as lucrative as being golden boy to Sir Chiffley Lockheart but I think I can just about afford sufficient oxygen to open my front door occasionally.

SANDY: Well what's the problem then?

KIRSTEN: There isn't a problem! It's just the principle of the thing, I just find grunters and honkers incredibly antisocial that's all . . . and when he laughs!! Great pneumatic snorts, just oxygenating the blood for no better reason than to grunt like a pig.

SANDY: He was laughing at my Stuttgart story which, as it happens, I told bloody well.

KIRSTEN: I wouldn't mind but I was blowing some really terrific stuff tonight, Sicilian, sucked on the

North face of Mount Etna, completely wasted on him of course.

SANDY: Oh for God's sake I hope you're not turning into a real air snob, I can't stand real air snobs, going on and on about this bloody air and that bloody air, it's all bloody air to me.

KIRSTEN: I don't believe this! I simply do not *believe* this! Who's been talking about nothing but air all evening!

SANDY: Well it's a bloody worrying time. There's a real free-trade backlash on the UK fixed-minimum gulp price, bloody Yank consortiums lobbying to bring in cheap air from bloody Africa, our stocks will be worthless . . .

KIRSTEN: I *know*, you haven't shut up about it for weeks!

SANDY: It's the bloody EEC. They *have* to subsidize European suckers, they're quite happy to subsidize wine lakes and butter mountains. The air industry's every bit as important to the European economy as farming, we must have air (*searches for the word*) . . . bubbles.

KIRSTEN: Look can't we shut up about it for one night?

SANDY (*getting up and grabbing coat*): Well if I'm being that dull perhaps I should just piss off then?

KIRSTEN: Perhaps you should!

SANDY: Right . . . (*at door*) Would you object *terribly* if I took a final big gulp? My car's a good fifty-yards away and your local council wafts at criminal levels.

KIRSTEN: Oh for God's sake Sandy, this is ridiculous.

SANDY: What?

KIRSTEN: I've been waiting for Geoff to go all
evening so you could give me a right bloody
seeing too, and now we're having a row.

SANDY: Well I'm sorry darling . . . you know,
pressure etc. . . .

KIRSTEN: I'm sorry too . . .

SANDY (*going to her*): Come here you ravishingly all
right bit of grappling fodder you . . .

KIRSTEN: Hang on, I'll just change the balloon on
the Suck and Blow; if we're going to be thrashing
and groaning and just having a ruddy good *bonk*
there's no point doing it to best Sicilian . . .

SCENE FOUR

Fade out as jets of steam shoot across the stage. CHIEF
and PHILIP, *towels round waists, having steam.*

CHIEF (*pouring water on a brazier of coals, provoking a
great waft of steam*): Do you know Philip, I've been
enveloped in most things in my time, from a
woman's arms to a bathful of raw mackerel, and I
still say there's nothing quite like the searing,
cleansing heat of the steam-room to brace a
fellow up.

PHILIP (*slightly preoccupied*): Uhm, no, absolutely Sir,
senior searing.

CHIEF: I must say I do sometimes allow myself a wry
smile when I hear it suggested that people like
you and I don't know what it's like to *really* sweat.
I mean, look at us now, positively evaporating. I
shouldn't think a coal miner would last much
above five minutes in here.

PHILIP (*still preoccupied, not really listening*): Absolutely
not, Chief, we'd have the grimy blighter thrown
out pretty sharp.

CHIEF: All right young fellow what's stuck in your
craw? Is it that girl from marketing? Getting

serious is she?

PHILIP: Chief, that's history, I walked, I was out of there. I said to her, I said 'listen lady, I'm dust, I'm a memory, don't look for me tomorrow baby because I'll be long gone.'

CHIEF: And what did she say?

PHILIP: She said 'all right' which I respected her for.

CHIEF: Do you know Philip, I've always seen it as rather a mistake to respect a woman, they see it as a sign of weakness.

PHILIP: We nearly had it all Chief, we were perfect for one another, everything was right except for the fact that she wasn't interested in me. That was the real problem and I just had no *time* to deal with that.

CHIEF: How could you have Philip? Your life's a Pot Noodle now. Look laddie, I've seen women every shape and every colour, but I've never met one yet who had a first-year turnover in excess of twenty billion.

(*He puts more water on the steaming coals.*)

PHILIP: Mmm yes, it's rather this Pot Noodle business that's been preoccupying me during our executive steam, Chief, and making me perhaps slightly less charismatic company than I might have hoped.

(*He puts more water on the steaming coals.*)

PHILIP (*pause*): Chief I wonder if you'd mind if I showed you something that's rather worrying me.

CHIEF (*worried*): Well I don't know Philip, I'm not a
doctor. I do know a fellow in Kensington who's
very discreet . . .

PHILIP: I've been sent this letter. (*fishes it out from
under towel*) It's got rather soggy I'm afraid . . .

CHIEF: A letter Philip?

PHILIP: Yes Chief, it's a kind of fax but there's no
telephone lines involved. It inputs via a slit in the
door, terrific concept . . .

CHIEF: I know what a letter is Philip. I'm constantly
receiving them from some people called
'Freeman's Catalogue', apparently with their help
I could look as good as Lulu. I confess I've always
found Lulu extremely attractive but then I find
trees attractive and I wouldn't want to look like a
tree would I? So where's the logic in that?
Anyway, what's so special about your soggy one?
Do we have a legal problem?

PHILIP: It's the reply that the American Indian
Chief, known as Seattle, sent in 1854 to the US
government on receipt of their request to buy
from him the land of his people.

CHIEF: You've been sent a letter by a dead Red
Indian?

PHILIP: No Chief, someone has anonymously sent
me a copy of the dead Chief's letter and it has
moved me Sir. I could not have been more
moved if I had been reading it on Concorde.

CHIEF: Sounds like potent stuff.

PHILIP: I truly believe that I would scarcely have been as emotionally affected by the contents of this letter if they had been written on a Stinger ground-to-air missile and fired up my trouser leg.

CHIEF: Strong reaction Philip. Tell me more.

PHILIP: Well, as I say, it concerns this old Tomahawk-twirling scalp collector named Seattle, who seems to have carried senior executive status over a predominantly hunter-gathering workforce operating out of Northern California in the middle of the last century.

CHIEF: Go on.

PHILIP: Well as I explained, he was memo-ing Washington *vis-à-vis* their purchase offer on certain choice properties of Red Indian real estate . . . Now this is his answer . . . (*he reads*) . . . 'Every part of the earth is sacred to my people' . . . (*stops reading*) . . . Amazing how little changes in corporate structuring eh Sir Chiffley? This fellow Seattle had his people just as you or I do . . .

CHIEF: The first rule of the jungle Philip, is to know how to delegate.

PHILIP: Every time Chief, and if you're too busy to delegate yourself then for God's sake get someone to do it for you.

CHIEF: Delegate, delegate, delegate. Wasn't it John Lennon who sang 'power to the people'?

PHILIP: Becoming the only major star in the history of rock to write a song about delegation within a management structure . . .

CHIEF: Small wonder the world remembers him.

PHILIP: Well quite. Anyway, as I was saying, Seattle has talked to his people and they have made a policy decision that (*refers to letter*) 'Every part of the Earth is sacred' . . . and now he is memo-ing the US Government on the issue. He continues . . . (*reads*) . . . 'Every shining pine needle, every sandy shore, every mist in the dark woods, every clearing and humming insect is holy in the memory and experience of my people' . . .

CHIEF: Holy insects?

PHILIP: Gripping stuff eh? (*he reads*) . . . 'We know that the white man doesn't understand our ways. One portion of land is the same to him as the next for he is a stranger who comes in the night and takes from the land whatever he needs. The Earth is not his brother but his enemy' . . .

CHIEF: I must confess Philip I have little patience with this fellow so far. The earth isn't a man's brother or his enemy, it's just the earth I'm afraid.

PHILIP: Oh I think it's more complicated than that Sir, hear him out, you'll find it's worth it . . . (*he reads*) 'The sight of your cities pains the eyes of the Red man. There is no quiet place, no place to hear the unfurling of the leaves in Spring or the rustle of the insects' wings' . . .

CHIEF: I can't say as how I've ever heard a leaf unfurl, have you Philip?

PHILIP: Incredibly acute hearing these Redskins, Chief. Just by putting their ears to the ground they could say how many riders were coming, how heavily they were armed and what they'd all had for dinner. Hearing leaves would have been junior stuff to them. Anyway, Seattle sticks with the theme (*carrying on reading*) . . . 'The clatter of your cities insults our ears, and what is there to life if a man cannot hear the lonely cry of the whippoorwill or the arguments of the frogs around a pond at night? If we sell you our land, you must keep it apart and sacred as a place where even the white man can go to taste the wind that is sweetened by the meadow's flowers' . . .

CHIEF: In which case there wouldn't be an awful lot of point in buying it would there? Look Philip, I'm sorry, but I simply don't see the relevance of all this to the air industry.

PHILIP (*pacing about*): Well Sir, as I originally saw it, the real excitement of our sucking operations was that we had found a way to tame the final element for the good of mankind, just as land and food and power and water and the very land itself had once been tamed.

CHIEF: Well I think that's a fair, if perhaps rather fanciful way of describing raking in a wadge of cash.

PHILIP: Then, when people started wandering around going purple and gasping for breath I thought, 'Whoops, hang on, hullo . . . I wasn't under the impression that going purple and gasping for breath was particularly high up on the list of things that are for the good of mankind.' . . . It struck me that it wasn't awfully long since everybody had had enough to breathe, and now, bugger me, but for the good of mankind, they hadn't any more . . . I mean old Seattle saw it coming with the land . . .

CHIEF: My dear Philip, I'm sure you'll forgive me but this fellow Seattle strikes me as being a bit of a turd. Throughout history there has always been some environmental luddite standing in the way of the natural development of a free-market economy.

PHILIP: Yes but . . .

CHIEF: If the United States legislature had so far shirked their responsibilities as to listen to this Seattle fellow where would the world's greatest democracy be now? Sniffing wind, listening to leaves and having arguments with the frogs, that's where.

PHILIP: You're right of course Chief . . . I just thought it might form the basis for a memo on policy development . . . After all, we do want our industry to be a valuable part of society don't we?

CHIEF: Of course we do Philip, as valuable as it can possibly be but there's only so much we can do to force up the price . . . (*steam*) You know Philip, I've been doing a bit of thinking as well.

PHILIP: Nothing like it eh?

CHIEF: Philip, you're my best man and I'm going to be perfectly straight. I think you're tired, you've

headed up the whole operation from the
beginning and you deserve a break. I want you to
take a break, so what do you say? Change of air?

PHILIP: I can get that at the chemist Sir.

CHIEF: I want you to take some leave Philip.

PHILIP: Well, I suppose . . . I don't know . . . I just
hate to see people go breathless, that's all.

CHIEF: Philip, it's a small portion of the population,
the vast majority are breathing cleaner, healthier
air . . . besides, the whole thing is a political issue.
It has nothing to do with us, we just provide a
service.

SCENE FIVE

Steam fills the stage, it clears. THE MINISTER FOR THE ENVIRONMENT *is making a speech.*

MINISTER: Of course we recognize that there is suffering and we will continue to seek out the truly deserving cases and provide them with all the help that they require . . . However, we believe that the onus lies partly with the less well off themselves to alleviate the problem. As with poor diet, we believe the main enemy is ignorance. In 1988 the Government issued detailed advice to the hungry on how best to gain sustenance. They advised in a leaflet issued through the Department of Health and Social Security that people should avoid treats and impulse buys, that they should not go shopping for food when they were hungry since this would lead them into unwise purchases. I feel that similar commonsense measures will help the less well off with their breathing. The plain facts are that some people are simply not breathing *properly*. For instance, is it really necessary for people to breathe quite so much? If you find yourselves in difficulties surely it would be possible to take shorter breaths. In the home, if

your income requires you to have your blower on
minimal output, try to move about less; silly and
wasted movements just use up precious
energy . . . Lie down on your bed and take slow,
well-spaced breaths . . . perhaps you could time
them. Avoid activities that you know will consume
air, keep family discussion to a minimum, don't
go upstairs if you can possibly avoid it, the
lavatory is a key danger, go only when you know
it's coming, any straining will throw your meter
sky high. Obviously love making is a very
irresponsible activity when the air is thin,
definitely to be avoided. Ask Grandma not to knit
so vigorously and get rid of the dog . . .

(*His voice is drowned by the roar of a jet.*)

SCENE SIX

Huge jet engine noises.

Front stage, KIRSTEN *and* SANDY *in two business-class British Airways seats.*

SANDY: Well darling, what could be more perfect, a combined honeymoon and business trip.

KIRSTEN: I couldn't believe it when Chief gave me the International Portfolio.

SANDY: Kirsten, the Chief knows I don't marry turkeys . . .

KIRSTEN: And he knows I don't marry men who marry turkeys.

SANDY: Touche Lady . . . tell you what, five hours fingering my lap top's put a right ruddy firework in my jocks. (*lap top down*) What say we bog up and join the Five Mile High Club?

KIRSTEN: Been there Sandy, believe me there just isn't room. I was 18, doing Europe, ended up with some Frenchman having to prise me off one of the taps. Maybe if your secretary had put us in first.

SANDY: Yes well she won't make that mistake again.

KIRSTEN: Good.

SANDY: No chance, I sacked her by fax from
Heathrow. But either way, first or business flying
is just a chore to me. I've cloud hopped a deal too
many flights to be spending my time saying, 'Oh
look how clever, they've managed to get the cod
mornay and the strawberry cream dessert into the
same container.'

KIRSTEN: Absolutely, anyway, it will be the best of
everything for us once we clinch the African deal.
Lucky for us Philip took leave, or he'd be heading
it up.

SANDY: Luck darling? Twelve types of hardly. The
guy needed a break. Some people bend, some
people snap, personally I'm a bender.

KIRSTEN: He had a good dream.

SANDY (*looking out of window*): Well it's certainly
going to come true for these African fellahs, I
reckon they'll strike a hard bargain. They've got a
phenomenal natural resource just waiting to be
sucked, I mean it'll be worth billions to their
economy. The Chief's told me to bid top dollar.
Incoming Third World air could totally undercut
European stockpiles. (*phone rings*) Sorry darling,
it's the new Foton Sattelite System, quite
superb . . . (*takes out portable*) . . . Yo Chief!! Well
this is a pleasure Sir (*adjusting tie*) . . . Marvellous
Sir . . . What? Uhm cod mornay and strawberry
cream dessert . . . Yes it is clever how they do that
isn't it . . . sorry? With all due respect Sir . . . (*to*
KIRSTEN) Pen, pen, pen . . . (*into phone*) Fire away
Sir . . . (*he takes down something*) Right you are

Sir . . . What? Sadly no Sir, Kirsten says the taps get in the way . . . Goodbye then Sir . . . Kind regards to Lady Chiffley . . . (*phones off*) Sod it.

KIRSTEN: So what was that about?

SANDY: Said he thought I might need Philip's advice on the African suck up . . . gave me the bloke's bloody number on the Costa Del Lager Lout . . . Well that's what I think of that! (*Screws it up . . . about to throw away, then slips in pocket.*)

KIRSTEN: Bloody cheek . . . (*film flicker*) Oh God the bloody awful movie . . .

SANDY: *Crocodile Dundee Four*, this is the one where he becomes President of the Soviet Union . . . It's great . . .

(*Plane off.*)

SCENE SIX (A)

Lights up on PHILIP *to side of stage in shorts and a sombrero, he takes a sip of wine and clicks a TV remote . . . There is a very low bluish flicker, as if he is watching TV . . .*

SCENE SEVEN

We hear a terrible buzzing of flies, people wailing, oxen snorting. BBC reporter with microphone wanders across front of stage. She has a backpack which feeds a tube to a big plastic bubble on her head.

REPORTER: These people are quite literally suffocating. The air is so thin that they find it difficult to find the energy to move . . . (*she appears to pick her way over something*) Of course there was a time when this region possessed oxygen in abundance. It still would have, were it not for the fact that the rulers of this tortured, divided country, both on the left and right, have systematically sold its resources for arms. Western developers, with the connivance of a corrupt administration, have sucked far beyond agreed international quotas. Now this region is all but uninhabitable. (*stops wandering about*) While this tiny child gulps painfully at the near empty and useless air, the oxygen that should be her rightful birthright lies unbreathed, far far away, stockpiled in order to protect the international gulp price. That she should be in such desperate straits whilst the means for her survival lies silent, invisible, useless, compacted down into the huge

Western Suck and Blowers, is vivid testimony of
man's inhumanity to man. (*she stops again*) This
goat did not die naturally, it was slaughtered by
the very people whose survival depends on its
milk and meat. The need for air supersedes even
the need for food and as the air thins animals are
slaughtered in order to stop them breathing and
consuming what little oxygen remains. (*motioning
around her*) This relief camp, jointly run by
Oxfam and War on Want, is currently supplying
breathing space for about four and a half
thousand refugees. They have struggled here,
gasping for breath from their homes in the
outlying hills where the air is now too thin for
survival. The scene is biblical in its horror. The
relief workers are operating three dilapidated
Mark One Lockheart Blowers at the centre of the
camp and people scramble desperately trying to
find a place near one of the outlets for
themselves and their children. The further away
one is, of course, the less chance there is of a
really good lungful. Added to this is the terrible
uncertainty that a sudden gust of empty wind will
carry off and dissipate the precious pumpings,
leaving the entire camp momentarily without the
means to live. Whenever even the slightest breeze
is felt, a great moan goes up and people huddle
closer, breathing deeply, bracing themselves for
the possibility of two or three minutes with
nothing to breathe at all . . . So far in this present
crisis over four million people have been
terminally suffocated or 'died' from the associated
problems of hunger and rioting . . . (*she addresses
the imaginary cameraman, brisk professional tone*) Did

you get the baby in Barry? The shot won't work
without the baby.

(*The* REPORTER *wanders off.*)

SCENE EIGHT

*A plastic tunnel stretches across the stage, the back half of
it anyway, obviously the front part is open for the
audience to see in.* SANDY *bustles on with the* CHIEF, *both
wearing hard hats.*

SANDY: Sorry I was late Chief, some bastard actually
  broke in and stole my air! Just whipped the
  balloon right off the sucker, I mean Christ that is
  sick! Bloody ironic as well, it must have happened
  while I was in the sitting room watching the ITV
  Breathathon . . . To think while I was trying to
  get through to the credit card hotline to let a
  baby breathe, some bugger was actually taking the
  air from right under my nose.

CHIEF: Yes, Lady Chiffley doesn't feel safe outside
  any more, there's so many people on the streets
  hanging about breathing . . . Apparently they
  can't afford to waft their own homes so they stay
  out half the night breathing public air.

SANDY: We saw you on the Breathathon though Sir,
  donating the Lockheart cheque, it was so great to
  see you with all those alternative comedians.
  Terrific for the company image. And so
  incredibly worthwhile. I couldn't believe it when

they cut to that beautiful little Sudanese baby and said our cheque would keep fifty thousand like her breathing for a year. Kirsten cried . . .

CHIEF: Yes, well it was a fun night and we're all proud to have done our bit to help, but we have work to do. How are we progressing with the breather tubes?

SANDY: Terrifically Chief, as you can see, we're well on course (*motioning round*). The tubes are fashioned from a fully translucent plastic substitute hence, while enjoying the air, the public user, be they a housewife going about her usual workaday routine, busy executive or overseas visitor, they will be afforded an unrivalled view of the on-street features and the shopping opportunities available outside (*showing it all off*).

CHIEF: Yes, well I must say it looks very smart.

PHILIP: Many thanks Chief, my people are good, damn good, there isn't one of them that isn't being individually groomed. The secondary advantages of the Breather Tube system need, of course, no explanation, so if I can just explain them, they are in the areas of civic cleanliness, and the prevention of civic skin cancer . . .

CHIEF: Sandy, the advantage of these tubes is that if you are inside one you won't suffocate.

SANDY: I'm certain they're going to prove an enormous earner. With councils cutting back so heavily on the strength of their atmosphere, anyone who can possibly afford it will choose to use the Lockheart Oxygenated walkways.

Entrance as you can see is facilitated by credit
card, so if Access and Visa want in they'd better
get ready for the pips to squeak . . .

CHIEF: Excellent. Excellent.

SANDY: Shops who want to be connected up to the
tube will of course have to pay massive rental on
their entrance . . .

CHIEF: And of course they'll all have to connect
because any halfway decent customer is going to
be in the first-class tubes . . .

SANDY: Uhm, actually I was speaking to Kirsten
about that term Sir, she felt the term 'first-class'
rather divisive and suggested the more user-
friendly 'Alpine class'.

CHIEF: I was not aware we had anything to
apologize for Sandy.

SANDY: Well either way Sir, I think a major back-
slapping session is in order Chief, these tubes
have definitely opened up another serious market
for Lockheart Oxy.

CHIEF (*snaps*): They haven't opened anything up! All
they have done is managed to recoup a little of
what we are losing through the never-ending cut
backs in oxygen consumption that our industry
faces every day . . .

SANDY: Yes but . . .

CHIEF: There are no buts, just facts. We have
developed these tubes in response to dizzy
shoppers demanding breathable air at street level.

SANDY: Exactly and . . .

CHIEF: And the reason that demand exists is because of Poll Tax capped councils cutting further and further back on the amount of oxygen they waft. Do you know what's going to happen next? I shall tell you, local councils are going to ask themselves, why, if the private sector can enclose the environment, can't they? They'll build their own civic walkways beside ours . . . The simple fact is that people are learning to live with much less air.

SANDY: Pretty chilling thought Sir.

CHIEF: I remember young Philip saying that the party was over a few months before he went on leave. I hope the poor chap isn't proved right.

SANDY: The guy just couldn't take the pressure of down-swing Sir.

CHIEF: The short-term solution is simple, we sell less air, but we charge more for it. I feel certain that the other members of the cartel will have no objections to raising the minimum gulp price. What happens in the long-term we shall have to ponder, but believe me, there is a recession coming, and when it does, it will be a cruel wind that blows and it won't bring any of us any good.

(*A huge wind is heard.*
The muffled crumps of explosions. The theatre flickers orange with flames, interspersed with bright red-orange flashes.)

SCENE NINE

CHIEF'S *office.*

The huge windows glow red, there are clearly enormous fires going on outside, occasionally there is a hot flash followed by a muffled crump. Obviously the effect should be dramatic. KIRSTEN, SANDY, *the* CHIEF *and* PHILIP *(possibly heavily sun-tanned). Perhaps another trolley of champagne.*

CHIEF: Well now Philip my dear boy, it's splendid to have you back on side.

PHILIP: It's good to be back Chief. I'm tanned, I'm fit, I'm raring like a rarerer.

CHIEF: I can't tell you how happy that makes me, you're my top man, you know that. Sandy's been heading up your presidency portfolio in your absence, but I know how delighted he'll be to hand the reigns back to you.

SANDY (*obviously not*): Delighted, Philip. It's a total pleasure . . .

CHIEF: Sandy's good Philip, damn good, but I need creative thinking at the very top. Some people discover Pot Noodles, some people make sure that they're stacked neatly on shelves. I think Sandy understands the difference.

SANDY (*a bit taken aback*): Well, I . . .

KIRSTEN (*defensively*): Sir Chiffley, I don't think that's . . .

CHIEF: So tell me Philip, you've been on the outside looking in for a while, what are your impressions of the situation. Not idyllic by any means I imagine.

PHILIP: Chief I'm a straight talking man, I'm not the sort of person to beat up a bush or waste words on mincers. The situation as I see it is serious.

SANDY: . . . Yes it's serious Chief, but with major plant closures . . .

KIRSTEN: . . . Strategic lobbying, saturation mail-shots . . .

CHIEF: Shut up Sandy, you too Kirsten. Philip's right, the whole industry has gone haywire, it's the 1973 oil glut crisis all over again. There is simply too much bloody air around.

PHILIP (*surprised*): Too *much* air Chief? Difficult to see that, I had to step over a couple of prostrate gaspers just between the car and the office.

CHIEF: Exactly. People aren't breathing enough of the bloody stuff. Philip my boy, it would be as well if we faced the facts squarely and like men. A combination of huge stockpiles and massively decreased demand have forced this great industry of ours into a vortex-like recession. It's time to face the music. I'm afraid it's going to be pretty unpleasant.

PHILIP: Bananarama time.

SANDY: Philip's right of course, the situation is bloody serious. Kirsten's been running background makes on . . .

KIRSTEN: Yes I've got Venn diagrams that will . . .

CHIEF: Young lady, when I'm up to my neck in shit I don't need a graph to tell me how deep it is . . . (SANDY *laughs sycophantically*, KIRSTEN *shoots him angry look*) There aren't many single industries big enough to create recessions that grow into full-scale *de*pressions . . . oil, automobiles, dieting, cosmetic surgery in the States . . .

PHILIP: Phew! You're right there Chief, I remember when Cher imploded. The whole industry collapsed. Let me tell you, when it comes to cosmetic surgery, if the bottom falls out, you might as well go home.

CHIEF: And likewise with air Philip; if we go down, the rest follows.

PHILIP: Nice to be up there with the big ones Chief. (*he crosses to the window*) I must say this African oxygen doesn't half burn.

SANDY: It should burn, the price Kirsten and I paid for it.

KIRSTEN: We had a marvellous trip, Philip. I brought you back a Nobbuck made out of dried bark and berries. It rattles when you shake it.

PHILIP: Hmm, yes, actually I've been meaning to ask you about this Chief. I mean, seeing as how it cost us so much and well, seeing as how the world is positively seething with purple faced gaspers, and I must stress here Chief, *children* are involved . . . is it actually really one hundred per cent necessary to burn so much oxygen? I mean, really?

CHIEF: Philip you know as well as I do that there is only one way to guarantee an adequate supply of oxygen and that is for the world to realize that if it wants to breathe it's going to have to accept reasonable pricing levels . . .

PHILIP: Hmm yes, but . . .

CHIEF: The only way we can hope to recoup some of the cost of total world sucking is to force up the price, and the only way to do that is to rationalize stocks. (*another huge glow and 'grump' noise at the windows*) . . . We can't sell the stuff, and having so much of it hanging around totally destabilizes the price . . .

PHILIP (*staring out of the window*): I still can't help feeling somehow that people could have breathed that stuff . . .

SANDY: Philip's been away a while Sir. I don't think he understands the new reality.

PHILIP: I think I'm looking at it Sandy.

KIRSTEN: The whole effect will look great on my corporate video. It'll really gee up the sales force.

CHIEF: Have you any idea how much grain was destroyed in the eighties Philip? While people starved, how much milk was poured away while babies screamed with want? Nobody likes it Philip, but you can't just give the stuff away; that way lies financial anarchy.

PHILIP: I admire your strength of commitment Chief. It would be so easy to make the obvious equation . . . People are suffocating: so burning oxygen is wrong. But you look further, you see the practical necessities of modern finance.

CHIEF: Somebody has to do it Philip. Anyway, there is actually a very real upside to our present burning programme.

PHILIP: There is?

CHIEF: Oh absolutely, now there's so little oxygen in the exterior atmosphere obviously it's not possible to burn anything . . .

PHILIP: Yeah, they've just disbanded Britain's last fire brigade.

KIRSTEN: I got some super nostalgia spreads in the tabloids . . .

CHIEF: So we've been able to do a rather decent little deal with the EEC agricultural cartel selling them our oxygen to burn their crops with. Now *that's* the sort of sound economics and good husbandry that keeps the world turning.

PHILIP (*still at window*): So there's food besides air in these fires?

SANDY: Damn right there is, how else do you think agri-business is to maintain a fair price for its product?

PHILIP (*thoughtfully*): The works of man upon earth eh? They have an awesome and majestic beauty.

CHIEF (*joining him at the glowing windows, arm on shoulder*): God created nature Philip, and man tamed it.

PHILIP: One hell of a partnership.

CHIEF: Yes but we haven't completely tamed the old fellow yet you know, he's still got a few tricks up his sleeve.

PHILIP: God?

CHIEF: Clever old sod. (*with test tube*) Just take a look at this Philip . . . it's green chlorophyll, the greatest enemy of the Oxygen Industry. This little natural vandal could, in time, destroy us and the jobs and revenue that we create.

PHILIP: Bugger me backwards Chief, it hardly seems possible: it's so small, so insignificant.

CHIEF: Well this isn't all of it Philip, obviously.

PHILIP: Isn't it? Oh I see, yes of course not Chief.

CHIEF: But there's a dollop of this in every leaf. In this. (*fingers the potted plants*) And in this. Every bit of green is packed with the stuff, and every day, whenever the sun shines, it whittles away, undermining the very basis of our great industry, threatening to cancel out the carefully regulated stocks upon which the gulp price is calculated.

PHILIP: But this must be quite awesomely worrying for you Chief.

CHIEF: It is Philip. Jemina. Mopsy. Janet over there. They're not just old friends any more. They are business competitors. Now think of our motor industry, well what would happen to it if nature started growing cars?

PHILIP: It would be knackered Chief.

CHIEF: Exactly, the situation has simply got to be regulated or else it will become impossible to set a price or manage the industry. It is possible to chemically manufacture oxygen, I see no reason to allow nature to do it . . .

SANDY: We have a global defoliation programme all geared up and ready to go. We've tested the chemicals on over a million beagles, and the last 100,000 or so survived more or less intact, so that should shut up the environmentalists.

KIRSTEN: I've been working on the trade justification campaign for weeks.

CHIEF: Obviously we can't do it alone, it will take world co-operation, but if the oil and motor industries can conspire against the cheap clean electric car in order to protect their expensive, dirty product, and the light bulb industry can sit on the everlasting bulb . . .

PHILIP: Painful.

CHIEF: . . . I see no reason why we shouldn't clear up this chlorophyll pest . . . (*snips the head off* JANET) Tscch. Business is business . . .

PHILIP: Chief, sorry to interrupt you when you're on a roll, but I think it's time I cut right through the bull's doodoo. Forget green chlorophyll, forget burning food mountains, we've got problems so huge you couldn't fit them into an elephant's trousers. Now I have an idea Chief, it's one I've been a-mulling for quite a time span. Interested?

CHIEF (*alert and interested*): Philip, it's a fool who thinks he's nothing left to learn . . . A fellow might wake up one morning thinking he's seen everything, and then he accidentally squats over a mirror and surprises himself. What's on your mind?

PHILIP: Well before I switch to explanation mode Chief, there's a degree of corporate restructuring that I'd like to implement in my capacity as President of the air division.

CHIEF: Carry on Philip.

PHILIP (*with his back to* KIRSTEN, *perhaps taking an off-hand interest in some portfolio*): Uhm yes, it appears that while I was away, we seem to have taken some rather expensive media wallahs onto the staff. I'm thinking particularly of the uhm . . . (*checks document*) ah yes, the Kirsten girl from Image Control . . .

KIRSTEN: Philip!

PHILIP: Chief I'm looking at shrinking demand, I'm looking at shrinking profit, this is a time for retrenchment not reckless expansion so I'm afraid we're going to have to let her go . . . (*turning round*) Kirsten, you're sacked.

KIRSTEN: Philip, I don't believe this, if this is just petty jealousy . . . !

PHILIP: Look, I don't have time for histrionics, lovey. Sir Chiffley and I have an entire air industry to turn round and frankly pretty adverts just ain't going to get the job done. Your desk has been cleared, the magnetic on your security laminate has already been wiped. You're out OK?

KIRSTEN: I don't deserve this Philip . . .

CHIEF: Harsh stuff Philip, I can't help feeling . . .

PHILIP: Chief, this is my Pot Noodle, I started it, I'm President of it and by buggery I'm going to build *my* team, with the people *I* want. Now if you have a problem with that Chief then fine, but there is no way I am telling you my brilliant new idea while that woman is in this room.

CHIEF: There's a new vigour to your staff relations Philip, I like it. (*to* KIRSTEN) Goodbye, we're all terrible sorry to see you go.

KIRSTEN: Sandy, say something!

PHILIP: Yes come on Sandy, say something. Which is it to be, the totty or the company? Don't dither.

SANDY: Uhm . . . I . . . well . . .

PHILIP: Chief that's the kind of dither span that could lose us upwards of a trillion yen on the floor in Tokyo. Get out Sandy, we'll discuss it later. Get out both of you, if I'm going to pull the Chief's irons out of the fire I don't need dead wood adding to the flames . . . (KIRSTEN *is at the door*) Kirsten, I want you to remember this.

(KIRSTEN *turns and looks, then turns on her heel and exits.* SANDY *makes a mute appeal to the* CHIEF, *he shrugs and nods towards the door.*)

CHIEF (*as they leave*): Quite a scene Philip. I hope your ideas justify the preamble.

PHILIP: Hope trade's pretty light on the international markets Chief, I sell certainties . . . I've been looking at the whole downside on the Private Air initiative and I reckon I've come up with my best idea yet. I'm *very* excited, so excited in fact that I haven't even told my people, I've brought the whole caboodle straight to the top. This is very much a between ourselves initiative Sir, we can take no risks of interference.

CHIEF: Now this really is exciting . . . (*back to desk, brisk and excited, he hits buttons*) Full security if you'd be so kind Miss Hodges, I believe we have a potential Pot Noodle in the building . . . (*more buttons and the same security measures as in first act happen, great metal screens on windows and doors etc. . . . of course the flaming flickering and 'crumps' from outside are now shut out, lights as normal*) All right Philip, we have maximum security, and you have my maximum attention.

PHILIP: OK Chief, as you know I've been pondering the world implications of our colossal Pot Noodle ever since the first pensioner turned purple?

CHIEF: Absolutely, and it does you credit Philip, it's essential to keep your eye on what I believe is currently called the downside.

PHILIP: Always watch the ground, what profiteth it a man to look to the top of the mountain if he's got dog do on his shoes. Anyway . . . for quite a while I was able to rationalize the major human-suffering downside of our industry . . . I accepted that some have more air than others, that profits have to be made . . . But I can't deny that I rather stuck on the mass suffocation bit.

CHIEF: But Philip, you've always been perfectly happy to live in a world that countenances mass starvation . . . mass homelessness . . .

PHILIP: Granted Chief, senior good point. It's just whereas you saw the example of food and shelter as justifying our air activities . . . I've rather come to see the air example as telling us something about food and shelter.

CHIEF: Rather tortured logic if I might say so Philip. In fact I'm not altogether sure I follow it . . . Have you got an idea or haven't you?

PHILIP (*excited*): Definitely Chief, no seriously, it's a whopper, a real whale's love weapon . . . Let me take you through its base line development.

CHIEF: I would be delighted.

PHILIP: Well, I was looking at the suffering, the recession, the poverty, the suffocation that I had been a large part of causing . . . and I had this huge idea . . .

CHIEF: Yes!

PHILIP: I thought, 'I know, I'll kill myself.'

CHIEF: By which you mean?

PHILIP: Kill myself.

CHIEF (*after pause*): . . . So it's not a metaphor? You actually mean, kill yourself, that's your idea?

PHILIP: Yes.

CHIEF: But for God's sake Philip, what are you saying? How can you blame yourself my boy, it was just good business, that's all, you're being stupid, foolish . . .

PHILIP: Well yes, I must admit that after a bit that's what I thought as well Chief.

CHIEF: I'm extremely pleased to hear it.

PHILIP: So I thought it would be better to kill you.

CHIEF: What!

PHILIP: But then I thought, Come *on* Phil, this is a brainstorming ideas session, let's apply some Larry logic . . . no point in killing the Chief, I thought, that would be absurd . . .

CHIEF: Good, excellent thought.

PHILIP: He's just one of many . . .

CHIEF: Well quite.

PHILIP: I should kill them all . . .

CHIEF: Now look Philip please, for goodness sake . . . !

PHILIP: No hang on Chief, let me stage-by-stage you on this one . . . Next I thought, this is just ridiculous, I can't possibly go and kill all the people who profit out of suffering . . . it would be impossible: in a way, we all do.

CHIEF: Of course, of course, thank heavens
you've . . .

PHILIP: So I went back to the idea of just killing you.

CHIEF (*after pause*): . . . Yes, and what did you think
then?

PHILIP: Nothing, I stopped there, that's it, that's my
idea.

CHIEF: But . . . but . . . you just said yourself it
would be pointless . . . !

PHILIP: I know, but I still think it's a good idea, even
besides that.

CHIEF (*hits intercom*): Security! Emergency . . . (*but the
intercom is useless as in the first scene*) Damn! look
this is . . .

(PHILIP *takes some heavy object, an award for industry
statuette and walks over to the gleaming high-tech Suck
and Blow with its beautiful balloon gently
breathing* . . .)

CHIEF: Philip no!!

(PHILIP *smashes it, dramatic flashes.*)

CHIEF: Philip that's our oxygen you stupid little
bugger!

PHILIP: It's still there Chief, I've just knocked out
the blower . . . Oh I forgot to say, I also went
back to the idea of killing myself . . .

(CHIEF *is at desk desperately punching buttons* . . .)

PHILIP: Come on Chief, you know the thing's on a
timer. We're going to suffocate, so forget it. Let's
think about something else . . .

CHIEF: You bloody lunatic!! (*shouts*) Help!
Help! . . . . . . (*turning back to* PHILIP) What the
hell's wrong with making a profit anyway . . .?

PHILIP: Well as I see it, there's profits and profits
(*having to support himself, bit gaspy*) I mean come *on*
Chief, surely you see, if you can't make a profit
without selling your soul then you shouldn't be in
business . . .

CHIEF (*staggering*): Of course you do realize you're
sacked don't you, completely and utterly sacked!
You're sacked, your people are sacked, your
people's people are sacked!!

(*He falls over.*)

PHILIP (*on knees*): Decision received and respected,
Sir! . . . I think you should memo it, the screens
won't lift for at least five minutes and we'll both
be gone in half that time . . .

CHIEF: No we bloody won't!

(*He crawls to windows, tries to force them.*)

PHILIP (*lying on back*): Senior waste of energy
Chief . . . Quite an interesting sensation really,
this is how most people feel all the time . . .

CHIEF (*at desk, gasping*): I'm going to survive this
Philip, and so are you, and when we do you're
going to realize what a hugely detrimental career
decision it is to try and kill your employer . . .

PHILIP (*lying on his back and gasping*): It wasn't made
lightly Chief, believe me, I was so unsure I nearly
rang my accountant.

CHIEF: Got it (*takes gun from draw*). We're going to make it you little bastard and when I've finished with you, you won't find a restaurant in WC1 that'll take your credit . . .

(CHIEF *staggers to windows and shoots at locks . . . 'bang' 'bang' 'bang' . . . 'click'. And with a 'whhhirrrr', the screens rise up again, revealing the flickering orange and red of the flames. Again we hear the crump of explosions.*)

PHILIP (*fading*): I'm drifting Chief . . . I want you to know that although I have come to despise both myself and you as men . . . I think we bonded into a bloody *senior* corporate entity . . .

CHIEF (*monumental effort, he has picked up the smashed Suck and Blow machine . . . he lurches towards the window*) I'll get some bloody air in here if it kills me . . . !!!

PHILIP (*nearly gone*): Air Chief?

CHIEF (*gasping*): Just . . . smash the bloody window . . .

PHILIP: Can't help feeling you're forgetting something here . . .

CHIEF (*huge effort raises machine above head*): We're going to live Philip!!! And when we do!! you bleeding heart liberal pansy, I'm going to kill you!

PHILIP: Chief it's empty out there. There isn't anything left to bre . . .

(CHIEF *hurls the machine through one of the windows.*)

CHIEF: Done it!! (*a wind howls in, papers blow etc., the noise of explosions suddenly huge*) Done it you bastard!

(CHIEF *stands, takes a huge gulp. Turns downstage to face the prostrate* PHILIP. *A triumphant smile which becomes glassy and transfixed as he can fool his lungs no longer and dies of suffocation.*)

(*The fierce wind blows and the lights flicker.*)

The End

'Every part of the earth is sacred to my people. Every shining pine needle, every sandy shore, every mist in the dark woods, every clearing and every humming insect is holy in the memory and experience of my people. We know that the white man doesn't understand our ways. One portion of land is the same to him as the next for he is a stranger who comes in the night and takes from the land whatever he needs. The earth is not his brother but his enemy. The sight of your cities pains the eyes of the Red man. There is no quiet place, no place to hear the unfurling of the leaves in the Spring or the rustle of the insects' wings. The clatter of your cities insults our ears, and what is there to life if a man cannot hear the lonely cry of the whippoorwill or the arguments of the frogs around a pond at night? If we sell you our land, you must keep it apart and sacred as a place where even the white man can go to taste the wind that is sweetened by the meadows' flowers.'

An extract from the reply that the American Indian Chief known as Seattle sent in 1854 to the US Government on receipt of their request to buy from him the land of his people.